Take Those Pants Off
And Put Your Bra Back On!

T. L. BROWN

Pink Leather Ink

Books for and about pretty strong women and girls

Dedication

For my future 18-year-old daughter. May relationships of 2030 and beyond meet all of your highest expectations. May the natural balance that is the trademark of true love be restored for the good of all humankind.
You deserve the best, baby.

CONTENTS

Take Those Pants Off
And Put Your Bra Back On!

==

Part 1
What Are You Wearing?

*I don't care how nice your pants are. They never look
as good on you as a dress.
Metaphorically speaking, of course.*

Take Those Pants Off And Put Your Bra Back On!

Introduction

It's simple. Very simple. If a man can't open a door for me, then I can't open my heart—or anything else he might want me to "open up" later on—for *him*. (Yes. Keep that mind in the gutter, because I definitely mean *"those"* and *"that"* too!)

That's my attitude when it comes to the modern male. Not that I'm some nose-in-the-air prima donna, but let's face it, chivalry is a turn on. And, by the contrary, nothing turns me off quicker than a man with no manners.

I'm just going to say it. These days it's as if some men feel as if we should be pulling out *their* chairs or telling them *their* hair looks nice. Asking for *their* hand in marriage. Sweeping them off *their* feet. Are they serious? Are *we* serious?!

Listen up, ladies. It's time we put an end to this nonsense. It's time we reassume our role as the chased, not the chaser. Kick off those cross trainers. Loosen up those laces. We're not men. We're not boys. We're women. Whether we sign our names with *Ms.*, *Miss*, or *Mrs.* it's high time we remember the prestige of those honorifics. It's time we know our value. Our worth. Our role. Not seeing ourselves as the prize has been our romantic demise. Our emotional, psychological, and material downfall.

It's time we get up. It's time we take back our power. It's time we own it. Exercise it. Right away! It's time we take our pants off and put our bras back on and demand some good old-fashioned chivalry in our love lives.

Not For You, *Boo?*

I am a woman who has made my fair share of romantic mistakes—*romanstakes*, I call them—including some of the things discussed in this book. This book is not for the woman who is perfect and has got it all together. Who never makes any mistakes or false moves with men. This is for the rest of us who, sometimes, fumble through romance, forgetful of our true worth.

Furthermore, it is not for the woman who already has an awesome, can-do-no-wrong, closest-thing-to-Jesus kind of man standing steadily by her side. It's for those of us who don't. *Hallelujah!*

Say It Ain't So, Sadie

We've all probably heard of Sadie Hawkins Day and its self-titled dances where the girls ask the guys out on this one-night-only event that occurs annually on November 15th. Perhaps it sounds exciting to change things up, to indulge in some role-reversing ritual for a single night in the name of fun. *What's the harm?* you might say. You want to get your *'Sadie On'* and take the beau by the horns. Fair enough. But before you pump that breath spray and slick your bangs back Fonzie-style as you prepare to approach your male target, are you aware of the backstory? Have you heard about the origin of this backwards, boy-chasing occasion? If not, the following is according to Wikipedia:

In *Li'l Abner*, Sadie Hawkins was the daughter of one of Dogpatch's earliest settlers, Hekzebiah Hawkins. The "homeliest gal in all them hills," she grew frantic waiting for suitors. When she reached the age of 35, still a spinster, her father was worried about Sadie living at home for the rest of her life. In desperation, he called together all the unmarried men of Dogpatch and declared it "Sadie Hawkins Day". A foot race was decreed, with Sadie pursuing the town's eligible bachelors. She was specifically interested in a handsome boy named Adam who was already in a courtship with a cute girl, Theresa, whose father was the area's largest potato farmer, Bill Richmand, and, unlike Sadie, had a number of courtship offers. Adam was invited to the race because Miss Theresa and Adam weren't actually engaged. With matrimony as the consequence of losing the foot race, the bachelors of the town were running for their freedom. Adam scored fourth place out of 10, leaving John Jonston as Sadie's prize. It is possible that the concept's origins are in an inversion of the myth of **Atalanta**, who, reluctant to marry, agreed to wed whoever could outrun her in a footrace.

"When ah fires [my gun], all o' yo' kin start a-runnin! When ah fires agin- after givin' yo' a fair start- Sadie starts a runnin'. Th' one she ketches'll be her husbin."

The town spinsters decided that this was a good idea, so they made Sadie Hawkins Day a mandatory yearly event, much to the chagrin of Dogpatch's bachelors. If a woman caught a bachelor and dragged him, kicking and screaming, across the finish line before sundown, by law he *had* to marry her.

Sadie Hawkins Day was first mentioned in the November 15, 1937 *Li'l Abner* daily comic strip, with the race actually being depicted between November 19 and November 30. It would prove to be an annual feature of *Li'l Abner*. (see Schreiner, Dave; "Sadie's First Run", *Li'l Abner Dailies Volume 3: 1937*, Kitchen Sink Press, Princeton, WI, p. 8.)

Is this the biography you'd like written about you one day? Do you want some much smaller-scale historian (aka your lousy ex-boyfriend) retelling a moment in time from *his* perspective where *you* were the reject running him down?

Listen up, Sadie! (Can I call you *Sadie?*) Every day is not the 15th. And every month is not November. So, let that story be a source of motivation—a cautionary tale—as you come along with me and get your "single and dating" act together.

But first, let's gauge your level of need. Let's see just how closely related you are to the seemingly self-loathing Sadie. Is she your fifth cousin, or your great aunt? Did you inherit her unappealing style of interacting with men? A victim of heredity, are your dating deeds dead ringers for Auntie Sadie's? Since we don't have either of your DNA readily available, let's assess your *"Guy-Q"* via a few questions to either rule in, or rule out, any possible relation.

Are you . . .

Book Smart, but Boy Dumb?

Take the quiz and find out.

Do you . . .

❖ Lead a team of 100+ employees but think men are superior to you?

❖ Spend more hours preparing for a date than it took you to finish reading *War and Peace*

❖ Pay for your own dinner on a date and then take him home for a little "dessert".

❖ Get excited when a man you barely know texts you at nine o'clock at night?

❖ Make decisions based solely on a man's desires?

❖ Want to cry when "So-and-So You Barely Know" doesn't call you in 3 days?

❖ Get jealous and competitive when your boyfriend tells you that other women have the hots for him?

❖ Believe a man's mouth instead of your own gut?

❖ Tell a guy how cute he is every chance you get?

❖ Believe *frustration + confusion + constant yearning = red-hot passion?*

Guy-Q Results

If you answered *Yes* to 3 or more of the questions, then you could certainly benefit from raising your Guy-Q, because there is a good chance that you, my dear, are Sadie reincarnated!

The good news is, unlike your IQ, your Guy-Q can be significantly raised in just the time it takes to read this book by following some simple, self-empowering steps. All it takes is for you to stay focused, be open to sound advice, and, most importantly, be honest. Seriously. You must let down your guard and be completely honest with yourself when reflecting on your dating style, habits, and experiences while reading this book. I promise that your most embarrassing secrets are safe here. So, go ahead. *Truth On!*

Rest Assured

If your Guy-Q is low, know two things:

1. You're not alone.

Many of us score below proficiency when it comes to knowing how to be successful with "He Who Has a Testicle or Two". We neglect to acknowledge our self-worth and, therefore, begin exuding characteristics and behaviors that are unflattering to us, and are counterproductive to our mission of connecting with a quality man with whom to cultivate a gender-healthy, female-friendly relationship.

2. It's not your fault.

Women have been conditioned. Brainwashed. Programmed to accept less than what we deserve. And, as you'll see, this conspiracy has been years in the making.

Part 2

What the (Bleep) Happened???!

Historical Perspectives in Getting Screwed

Sometimes you have to dig in the dirt to really clean things up.

.

Take Those Pants Off And Put Your Bra Back On!

Feminism Gone Wrong 101:

Splitting Tabs, Burning Bras, and Other Bad Ideas

Time for a little history lesson, ladies.

America. 1914. The war left women lonely.

Or did it?

Yes, they were without their husbands, but if we consider the quality of some of those marriages (and spouses) then maybe, for some, that was a good thing—for *both* parties.

With the breadwinners out of the house, for better or for worse, women were left to fend for themselves financially. What did they do? They said *Bring It On!* and went to work. Many of them loved it. They loved the freedom that financial independence afforded them. Some of their marriages felt like prisons. Still, others just liked the sense of personal pride, success, and accomplishment that went along with being self-sufficient. That was all great stuff. But then, somewhere along the way, things changed.

Decades later these courageous women had descendants in the mix. Their grand- and great-granddaughters, armed with a little self-made dough in their cute little handbags, started feeling themselves. *Ourselves.* Because "they" are *us.*

We started imitating men, believing that being like the guys made us more powerful, stronger women. Rather than acknowledging the fantastic strength of our femininity in its own right we tried to replicate masculine energy. And that never works out well. How did that happen?

Usher in the 90s...

I love 90s pop and fashion just as much as the next person. Baggy pants and colorful shirts were just coming onto the scene when the Fresh Prince of Bel-Air had everyone running to the malls to cop his cool duds. Clothes were flashy. Hair was high. And music seemed louder than ever before.

But while many little girls were grooving with their pink little boom boxes, listening to N-Sync, New Edition, and Savage Garden sing their gentlemanly way into millions of tweenage hearts, other, less gentlemanly recording artists expressed creative differences as they related to their thoughts about women and the appropriate dynamic of male-female relationships. While breakdancers were drawing large crowds at Venice Beach, these less-than-lady-loving lyricists and their chewed number two pencils on spiral notebooks were busy breaking *us* down.

Songs like *Bitch Betta Have My Money* helped set off a chain reaction of disrespect and misogyny. (And, no, he wasn't saying *'have'* as in *"Help yourself to* my *money, my dear. My mula is your mula"*. Not by far. He was, rather, demanding that the woman pay him for sex.) Similar messages began pumping through the walls of our favorite nightspots. And this was only the tip of the iceberg. Surely, we can't forget about *Shake That Ass Bitch and Let Me See What You Got, Big Pimpin', Ain't No Fun (If The Homies Can't Have None), There's Some Hoez In This House, Me So Horny.*

You get the picture.

Initially, these outrageous songs were isolated to a small audience, a narrow demographic, but soon their sordid sound waves permeated the air of even some of the poshest night spots, invading the orifices of partygoers from big cities to rural towns and communities.

Stealthily, these offensive, barbaric lyrics came bundled with beats that were hypnotizing and, sadly, inspiring. Worse than the worst subliminal message, these female-bashing beats took over our bodies and made us want to get out there and dance. Women, that is. Men just stood back and watched us bring the songs to life.

So we found ourselves huddled on the dance floor, dancing with ourselves, holding our self-purchased drinks, shaking our pretty little behinds compliantly, all the while giggling and making googly eyes at the menfolk standing on the outskirts nodding their heads in superior approval, assuming that we *must* be down with the musical message washing our brains. *'Wow! Look at that bitch over there shaking her ass and letting me see what she's got. Shake it, bitch! Shake it!'*, was what they had to be thinking, because there we were, obeying Splack Pack and Kid Money's orders, shaking our asses and letting them see what we've got.

But degrading lyrics and the 90s weren't the end of it. For there was more misogyny on the horizon. As the 90s prepared to wrap up, unbeknownst to us, there was more mayhem in the works. And it wouldn't be long into the next millennium before we'd see the emergence of low-quality literature getting in on the act. We'd soon see male-targeted books like *How To Be A Player* filthy up the shelves of some of our favorite bookstores, muscling their way into the Self Help sections, taking up precious reading real estate on cherry oak planks.

So be it via the radio or our favorite reading rooms the 90s (and immediately following) found us *out* with our girlfriends, and *in* with ourselves, awaiting instructions on how to proceed into the next millennium. Goodbye 20th century.

Then came Y2K...

When the 90s showed itself to the door, looked over its shoulder, and told us *'It's been fun'*, we waved back ambiguously, wondering whether we should thank it, or punch it in the face. You see, we were still dissatisfied with our love lives. We weren't any better off than we were before all the booty-shaking and drink-buying. And now, to top it off, we didn't feel accomplished enough. Or pretty enough. Or smart enough. We felt like there was still so much more work to be done before we could dare consider ourselves worthy of love. Not just any love. The kind of love movies told us existed in the worlds of *other women*. Women who were not us. Women we wanted to be. We decided we needed to up our game. We needed to figure out ways to make ourselves more romantically marketable in order to secure a guy like 'whatever those perfect women's names are that they tell us exist'.

Determined to make ourselves a "certified catch" —even if it killed us—we began burning ourselves out. We found ourselves getting up at the crack of dawn, rushing off to work with our college degrees on display, designer suits on our backs, and power pumps on our feet, clutching purses that we'd spent so much money *on* that we couldn't afford to put much money *inside*. We worked until the sun was about to set, then, worn out, hopped back into our cars, checking for messages from "You Know Who, Who Did <u>Not</u> Call."

We thought he liked us. How *couldn't* he? We'd put our best pedicured foot forward with him, hoping he was The One. We'd cooked for him. Told him all of our business in order to show just how attractively-layered we are. We slept with him. Put it on him in the *best* "worst way" in the bedroom. So, why didn't he call?

After pondering it for a few weeks we soon realized that he *was* The One. The One who didn't want us. The One who wouldn't call us back. The One who'd already had his way with us and was now moving on to the next long-legged adventure. The One we wanted to murder!

Feeling the rejection, but not really wanting to risk spending a lifetime in a 6 x 8 cell, followed by an eternity in hell, we replaced our homicidal fantasies with modified hope, and began exploring Plan Bs. All the while, though, we were hurting. Struggling. Self-doubting. The pain, as intense as it was, tried to get our attention. And eventually it did. It made us think. That was a good thing. The pain told us that something was off, and that we needed to take some time to rethink our romantic strategies, our choices when it came to dating "Mr. *'F You!'* For Not Calling", and the likes of him in other men, as it had now been revealed to us that there was a high risk of heartbreak associated with exercising poor judgment and dating a dirtbag.

Dating a dirtbag is dangerous. It can seriously injure your self-esteem.

Again, this pain-driven pondering was good. Reflection is a wonderful thing. But instead of responding to this pain, this stimulus, in a way that would've easily corrected things we started over thinking things. Like when you overthought that relatively easy multiple-choice question back in AP Human Geography. The one whose answer you *knew* but it seemed too easy, too simplistic to actually be correct. Putting our magnificent brain power to poor use, we overanalyzed the obvious. Nonetheless, being the natural problem-solvers that we are, we sashayed our way back over to our respective drawing boards and began drafting plans for a comeback. A stronger, pain-proof comeback.

Become the predator, not the prey! was what we came up with. We psyched ourselves out to believe that we could operate as men do and, thus, be happier. Or, at least, less sad. *Be like the boys!* we encouraged each other. *If we can't beat them, <u>be</u> them!* we thought, sure that we'd cracked the code of conduct that would bring us ultimate dating success. Lil' Kim told us we could be Boss Bitches who could run the whole sexual show and have him eating out the palms of our hands while keeping our emotions and egos in check. Even Destiny's Child had us thinking we could coldly *"When-It's-All-Over-Please-Get Up-and-Leave"* him, as we roll over onto our sides for some extra shuteye and bask in a more masculine version of afterglow, telling him to lock the door behind him on his way out.

While that *"Brr-*lesque" strategy may work for the World-famous, Multi-talented, Filthy-rich, and Beautiful combo—The *WMFB*—as it applies to the rest of us, being so icy will only leave us lonely. In plainer English: it ain't gon' work for us. Sorry. It's just not. Because his ass *will* get up and leave, which would be fine if that's what we really wanted. But since it isn't, well, as any responsible sword swallower would say, don't try that at home.

For those of us that actually *want* our man of the moment to stay, to hang around for a while, that *kiss and dismiss* strategy would work against everything that we hope for in a potential relationship. We want him to stay. We want him to stay and love us. We want him to be our mate. Dismissing him is the furthest thing from our minds after we sexually connect with a guy we like. And trying to play cold-hearted, overriding our natural instincts—our marvelous Mother Nature-provided programming—to behave as if we can operate on an emotionally-absent level as some of these male "players" do is just us, now, playing *ourselves*.

Nonetheless, some of us did try this strategy . . . and failed miserably. The whole trying to act as if we lacked emotions subsequently made us even bigger victims of bad romances and left us even sadder than we were before. Here's why:

We're NOT men.

That's a biologically simple fact. Just like we are not ducks, we are not men. We'd look quite silly waddling around the city, quacking like crazy because we thought ducks had it better, now wouldn't we? Likewise, we look equally as absurd trying to pull off the same stunts as some of these so-called men and believe we'll actually experience increased satisfaction and relationship success. Beaks off, Beauties! We're women. Let's work *that*!

Songs That Uplift Women—and *Love*

Tired of self-esteem-lowering songs in your diamond-studded satellites? Try these alternatives, sure to give you an instant boost, and remind you of just how precious of a being you really are, and what *real* men think of you and our kind.

Some of us may call these corny. No worries. That's just the brain-washing talking. You'll work through it. Eventually, you'll come to find that the word you're actually looking for is "decent", or "loving", or "beautiful". Maybe even "what used to be the norm before all the brain-washing and manipulating". And don't just stop at the titles. Listen to the lyrics. *Enjoy.*

A Decent Dozen

1. You Are So Beautiful – Billy Preston

2. I love You Just The Way You Are - Billy Joel

3. I'll Name The Dogs – Blake Shelton

4. All My Life - K. C. and Jo Jo

5. I'll Never Break Your Heart - Backstreet Boys

6. This I Promise You - N' Sync

7. Endless Love - Lionel Richie

8. I'll Make Love To You - Boys II Men

9. I Don't Want to Miss a Thing - Aerosmith

10. When a Man Loves a Woman - Percy Sledge

11. She's Got a Way - Billy Joel

12. I Just Called To Say I Love You - Steve Wonder

So, What About That Bra-Burning Business?

The Women's Liberation Movement

On the historical heels of the women's "right to vote" victory, The Women's Liberation Movement was like round two of *"Get Your Foot Off My Neck!"* and was comprised of several feminist groups who continued to fight against all forms of oppression and male supremacy. They fought for equality with respect to politics, personal choices, and economics. Without it you and I would be living a substantially less-quality life today. Here were some of its victories for us women:

- the right to work

- the right to NOT be fired for being pregnant

- the right to pursue a higher education

- the right to play college sports

- the right to study W*omen's Studies*

- reproductive rights

Way to Go, Ladies! Great Job! And THANK YOU!!!!

Imagine living a life where the above was *not* the norm. Pretty repulsive, right? Yep. Oppression always is.

Yet, while the Women's Liberation Movement set out to undo some of the lousy laws that the breast-and uterus-less population had established, it did not, however, fight for the following reasons:

Dear Miss Independent,

The Women's Liberation Movement set out to liberate you from oppression and inequality, not to liberate you from your good, God-given sense.

• to make you believe that you should be the one to ask a guy out on a date

• to give you the impression that you should pay for said date

• to encourage you to call a guy, or text him like crazy

• to compel you to compare yourself to other women, or to compete for the affections of a man

- to have you criticize yourself every time you look in the mirror

No, my lovelies. Those wonderful warriors of women's rights did not fight for your right to be a fool, or to let a man walk all over you. Nor did they fight for you to begin *becoming* men or behaving like them. Otherwise they would've called it the Women's *Termination* Movement. Stop playing "The Adam's apple". Stop trying to emulate men. Stop trying to prove your strength and just be strong.

A woman is strong, not because she can "act" like a man. She is strong because she is a woman!

A man after my own heart, William Golding said it best:

"I think women are foolish to pretend they are equal to men. They are far superior and always have been. Whatever you give a woman, she will make greater. If you give her sperm, she will give you a baby. If you give her a house, she will give you a home. If you give her groceries, she will give you a meal. If you give her a smile, she will give you her heart. She multiplies and enlarges what is given to her. So, if you give her any crap, be ready

to receive a ton of shit!" – William Golding, British Novelist, Playwright & Poet, 1911 – 1993.

The Bras? The *Bras* Already? What About The *Bras?!*

Headlines of barbecued bras strategically stole the show, subtracting from the seriousness of the Women's Liberation Movement. News reports of women taking off their boob-holders in support of the movement was disproportionally prevalent, intentionally eclipsing and minimizing the real goals of this very powerful, momentum-gaining fight. Rather than real coverage, some media outlets broadcasted their own versions of the movement, thus manufacturing it in the minds of the masses.

Their versions painted these very courageous women marching around taking off some piece of their lingerie in the name of liberation and equality and burning it on the streets in a freedom-demanding display. This, sadly, for some, became what first comes to mind when thinking about the social-political movement.

While there was a very small group of women protestors who, on one particular day, outside the Miss America contest, threw several items into a trashcan, including some bras, the term "bra-burning" associated with the Women's Liberation Movement was a gross misrepresentation of what was really going on. This was clearly an attempt to discredit and ridicule. And it was later revealed that no burning of *anything* ever took place that day, bras included. This "fake news", as we'd call it today, was just another way to make women look silly and unworthy of being taken seriously.

So, before you go unhooking your racerback, consider that you and I have been brainwashed into believing that the strong, courageous, socially-conscious women before us rallied primarily for the ridiculous right to go braless. It's just not true. Don't believe the hype.

Just as the old school media tried to make the world believe that bra-burning and going braless was the central focus of the Women's Liberation Movement, modern, manipulative men will have you believe that paying your own way on dates, and carrying *his* load, is the new norm. It isn't. So, go on, "put your bra back on", and adopt reasonable, high standards when it comes to dating. It's still reasonable to expect to be doted on by a man who is interested in getting romantically close to you.

Being a woman with standards is always in fashion.

In Part 4 of this book we will discuss more about what it means to put your bra back on as well as fantastic ways to do so.

His-Story

As we saw in the previous section, our mindsets as they pertain to dating and relating to men have sustained some serious trauma. It's fair to say that history hasn't necessarily been women's best friend.

Men, too, however, have a history of their own worth telling. There is certainly a historical perspective to be considered when it comes to our testosterone-rich counterparts. Men, it seems, have a history of busying themselves, as well as being obsessed with speed, capture, and collecting.

When a man is a boy he has hobbies to which he devotes his time, energy, and resources. He'd spend his allowance on his interests, and his weekends in the garage working on his favorite pastimes. Trains, coin-collecting, amateur etymology. He finds delight in these things. As he ages (Notice I didn't say *matures,* as that is not necessarily a given, as is *aging*) his focus shifts. He develops a new hobby. A new focus: You.

Us.

Women!

Women become a man's favorite new hobby. His fascination revolves no longer around objects with wheels and wings, rather bodies with boobs and softer things. His obsession with speed now relates to how fast he can get into your underwear. No longer do the males of our species upon growing up try to capture bugs and collect old currency. When their bones elongate and facial hair sprouts, so, too, do their appetites for capturing your sweetest affections. They're, now, more interested in having their way with you, and then bragging about their conquests over brewskies with the boys. Yes, women become men's favorite hobby. The hobby of all hobbies.

Yes. It's all about you. Go on. Blush. But this isn't just an ego-feeding exercise. No false sense of self-importance being dished out here. Just real deal, true blue facts. A single man spends the majority of his time, whether he recognizes it or not, making decisions that better position him to appear more desirable to women. From his haircut to his car. From his job to his gym, he wants to increase his chances of meeting a fantastic woman. (That's normal, by the way. And we *like* that, don't we? - Let's all shake our heads in unison.) So while we're reminding ourselves of that fact, let's remember this as well: It only works to our benefit if we know it to be true, and if we play our role accordingly. Because . . .

The one who is pursued has the power.

Now let's clear up any negative connotation associated with the word *power* because I don't want this to get in the way of how you receive this message and, thus, deny what is rightfully yours. We must do this right away lest we proceed with an unwarranted aversion to this idea, and an unwillingness to assume this gift that is inherently feminine.

Power is not a bad thing. It's not some sadistic tool we wield in order to degrade or disrespect another person. So, guys, (if you're nosy enough to be thumbing through this right now) don't get your boxer briefs in a bunch. (And while we're at it, put this back on your woman's shelf!)

Power, as defined by Webster's, is the following:

1 a : possession of control, authority, or influence over others
2 : ability to act or do something
3 a : physical might **b :** mental strength

All of those definitions work for me. How about you, ladies? *You* have the power. Stop forfeiting it. *You* are the prize. Nature made it that way. Males work toward winning over females. They pursue. They prance around. They chase. They impress. They provide. Don't believe me? Just take a glance around the animal kingdom. Take birds, for example. Let's look at some of the things male birds do for the love and attention of a female.

They Sing Their Hearts Out

Sexual selection can be as fickle as hitting the right note at the right time. And while singing when it comes to birds is not all about attraction, it's hard to deny that, as a female, being sung to is a pretty darn good aphrodisiac, and, in this case, a fairly effective way for a male bird to get a peak under those feathers.

They Get Their Dance On

Male birds really know how to cut a rug. But even if they aren't the Fred Astaire of their flock that doesn't stop them from trying to dance their way into the love nests of the females of their species. Crested pigeons, albatross, and bower birds, to name a few, all bust a move in the name of lure. Birds-of-paradise, in particular, take their choreography quite seriously. They don't just rely on those fancy dance genes that they inherit by the dozen from Papa Paradise, but actually spend significant time practicing to refine their moves in order to really make them their own. How could any female resist?

They Gift

Penguins, like some other birds, are so serious about winning the object of their affection that they show the female of their choosing that they are able to provide for them in a major way. Male "pengs" present to their chosen ones beautiful stones and pebbles as a way of saying "Baby, I can get this ice off your ass. Let's build a home together". He then uses these geological gems to build her a nest in which the two of them share. Cool move.

Not to be outdone, though, spiders have taken a page from the Penguin's *Lovers with Blubber* Handbook and did some slight editing. Instead of pebbles and stones, spiders of the species *Paratrechalea ornate*, for example, will present to their courted ones silk-wrapped yummies in order to get a little eight-legged lovin'. While she's busy unwrapping her din-din, he's "goin' in". But, as with all spiders, you really have to watch your back. Some of their "prey presents" —up to 70%— turn out to be total duds (his leftovers, random scraps, and offerings of very low nutritional value). It's like giving her a fake diamond.

Where's the bug spray when you need it?

They Show What They're Working With

No male of our species would ever wish to be referred to as being "hung like a bird". But in the case of the Ribbon-tailed astrapia this little birdie would be considered the most well-endowed of all birds, relative to its body size. Its 3-foot-long pair of tail feathers proves effective at turning plenty feathered heads. While toting around such biological baggage can be a, literal, pain in the rear for him, as it makes him more visible to predators and often gets tangled up in tree branches, the payoff is in the preferential attention he receives from the lady birds. Putting sex before safety, he wouldn't be the first male of *any* species to risk his life for a piece of punani.

They Make the Ultimate Sacrifice

This one's not exactly bird-specific, but it's certainly worth mentioning. While some birds are known to mate for life, such as the Bald Eagle, Black Vulture, and California Condor, a certain insect takes their "til' death do us part" promises to a more drastic and premature level. Upstaging all other males of the animal kingdom, praying mantis males allow themselves to be eaten mid-mating. Yes, eaten! But even though he won't be around to change any "mini mantis" diapers, Daddy still brings home the bacon, so to speak, as these males make for an excellent source of nutrients for the eggs the female will lay as a result of their copulation and her subsequent cannibalization of him. So while having his head bit off while getting his swerve on doesn't exactly seem very romantic, this papa-to-be takes posthumous pride in being able to still provide for his youngins' in the afterlife. Whether it costs a, literal, arm and a leg, kids gotta eat! Talk about crumb snatchers!

Bird and bug envy? Yeah, me too. But don't fret. It's not too late to learn from our fellow females, feathered or otherwise. We're not asking for the males of our species to go all "praying mantis" on us, but maybe a little "penguin" would do the trick.

Are You In?

So now that you've got a little background and a better understanding of the mess that's become of the human dating ritual, let's get started on fixing it. Ready? I'm with you, ladies. We're in this together. Come along with me as I inspire you to take those pants off and put your bra back on in order to resurrect some *real* love in our lives.

Part 3

7 Steps to Taking Off Your Pants

A man can't pull out your chair if you've already pushed in his.

#1

Stop Paying

Take Those Pants Off And Put Your Bra Back On!

Dutch???

No Thank You Very Much!

There is absolutely no reason why you should pay to let some guy spend time basking in your company. To that, I say the five following words:

Put your *bleeping* purse down!

If he's strapped for cash, do free stuff. Go to the park. The beach. Grab your water bottles and go for a hike. Go to the museum on a day there's no admission cost. The library. Bird-watching for a little dating inspiration. Anything except footing the bill for the both of you, or even for just yourself.

A man wouldn't expect his own mother, or sisters, or future daughters for that matter, to assume the role of Daddy Warbucks and bankroll brunch for two. You don't even have to explain this one in order for him to understand when it comes to the women in his life that he loves. So don't let him get all liberal with you while being conservative with his cash. Only a selfish, disrespectful cheapskate would allow a woman to pay for their first days or nights out together. He'd have to be a bona fide bozo to expect such a thing. *Clueless* or *Classless*, neither of which make for suitable partners. You don't need a guy like this one finding his way onto the precious pages of your datebook.

I recognize that for some women this may be a hard sell. And to those women, I'd ask the following:

What is so sexy about a stingy man?!

Seriously. What is attractive about a guy who is not willing to chase you with whatever he has? What is so irresistible about a member of the male gender who is perfectly willing—content, even—to sit back and let a woman foot the bills? Where is the turn on in that scenario? The only turn on there for me is me turning on my heels to head in the opposite direction of that man.

Now you may say you don't need his money. You may argue that you make all the money you need, and that you don't want to muddy the waters with this man by making an issue of money. You figure you make enough to treat the two of you, because it's not about the money, after all, it's about the love. The *money-ain't-a-thing-so-long-as-I-have-my-job* kind of love.

My response: *Don't* make an issue of it. By all means, make your money.

Make. Your. Money. *Honey!*

But just because you have a surplus of cash doesn't mean that you should start paying for. . . *attention.*

Yeah. "Attention". That's the word I was looking for.

Attention:

Flashy-Cashy Girls,

Get a Grip!

Put your wallet up, woman! Don't get suckered into adopting the lame philosophy of *"I make my own money, so really don't need a man to pick up the check on a date"*. No, I say! Let him pick it up   anyway. Let a man prove to you his level of interest in all the ways that men have proven their levels of interest t wonderful women before us. You deserve it.
Well, can I, at least, splurge on him? Buy him clothes, shoes, and tech gadgets?

Let me say it in Spanish this time: *No!*

A man should still work for your attention and affection. We shouldn't lose that ritual. We shouldn't change the rules of the game just because we have a little more money in our checking accounts. A man still needs to be a man. And a woman still needs to let him. A man still needs to want you more than you want him in the beginning. And he should still demonstrate this through his actions, one of which being picking up the tab. The *total* tab. Trying to split things down the middle during the honeymoon stages of a courtship just sucks out all the fun of being courted in the first place.

Courted. He should be courting you. *Court-ing!*

Let's define that word. Shall we?

Courting (v.) –

Function: *verb*
1 a : to try to gain <*court* favor> b : to act so as to invite or provoke <*court* disaster>
2 : to seek the affections or favor of <the candidate *courted* the voters>
3 a : to engage in a social relationship usually leading to marriage b : to engage in activity leading to mating <a pair of robins *courting*>

The first thing to point out is that *courting* is a VERB! This means there is, and must always be, action involved. Actions, as we all know, speak louder than words. Talk is cheap. Actually, talk is *free*. And anybody can do it. Whisper those sweet nothings all you want, but it's "put up or shut up" at the end of the day.

Money, as we know as well, is a very important resource. And the act of a man spending his on you is a wonderful verb if I ever knew one. (*Spending* is a verb too.)

Knowing how important money is in this world to every individual, it goes without saying that a man willing to spend his hard-earned income on you can be a pretty decent indicator of just how far he's willing to go to get to know you. How badly he wants to spend time with you. How much he wants to please you. It's certainly not the be-all end-all. But it's definitely a great start. A lovely little litmus test, if you will, of his potential love (or—heads up—*lust*) for you.

Guilt-Free Standards

Don't let recording artists contend with your womanly intuition. Resist the urge to allow catchy lyrics to serenade you into stupidity. Hold your standards high with confidence in the belief that if a man asks you out it is perfectly normal for you to expect to be treated to a meal, movie, or other date-appropriate adventure. And don't let some penny-pinching punk make you feel guilty for it.

But Doesn't That Make Me a

Gold Digger?

Hush your face, No! (That's not just an ordinary *No*, but a don't-be-ridiculous—slap-yourself-for-even-*thinking*-so—*No*.)

A person is dubbed a gold digger for their sole romantic interest in money, jewels, etc. What's more, the term *gold digger* is also 1) most likely male-invented, and 2) often misused.

In spite of the above, let's spend just a moment on this particular kind of person.

Gold diggers are those individuals who, instead of love, are in pursuit of profit. Rather than romance, their radars are set to scope out situations and relationships that can provide for them monetary and material gain. They have an isolated interest in what financial resources another person can bestow upon them in exchange for their attention and/or affection. This is typically someone who couldn't care less about the rest of the individual she is allowing to pursue and entertain her. One who would probably settle for less when it comes to more important qualities and personality traits so long as the man has money that he is willing to spend on her. He doesn't necessarily have to have a lot of it in every case. He just has to be willing to spend whatever he does have on her.

There is nothing wrong with a woman who appreciates a man spending money on her, just as there is nothing wrong with a man appreciating the company of a beautiful woman (as opposed to one he isn't physically attracted to). People have their personal preferences. In the case of a so-called gold digger, however, usually there is some form of callousness or deception that accompanies one's desire for their courter's cash. For example, a woman telling a man she loves him when, in fact, she doesn't. Something like this would, of course, be frowned upon by those of us who find this not only deceptive but unethical in every sense.

On the other hand, some gold diggers may be very transparent and upfront about their interests being "target locked" on a man's pockets. And, just as plain, the man may be perfectly fine with this for his own personal reasons and pursuits. Different things float different people's boats.

(Note: Men can be gold diggers as well. But this book is written for women. Now, as we were.)

In either case, when we talk about a gold digger we're talking about someone who, usually, doesn't care a smidgen about the man she is with. She is only with the man for his money, nothing more. End of story. What I am writing about in this section is entirely different. And it's certainly not a new concept. A man should still be expected to pick up the tab on dates when courting a woman. And a woman should not feel as if she is behaving like a gold digger, or anything else derogatory, by having this expectation. Besides, I've never heard of anyone calling a man a "beauty digger", or "sex digger".

For the Record

Let me say that I am not advocating for the exploitation of any man, or any human being for that matter. I'm not telling you to go out and use a man until he's all used up. I'm telling you to know your worth, and to let a man know it through your actions, or inaction. Let him know that you have a certain standard set for yourself as it applies to any man interested in getting close to you. This is your right. He has rights, too, by the way. He has the right to leave you alone. He has the right to not ask you out on a date. He has the right to look elsewhere for his romantic needs and curiosities, and to stay the heck out of your lovely face. God Bless America!

A man who doesn't want to woo you, but only wants to screw you, doesn't see any real value in you. Therefore, you shouldn't be seeing him at all.

Now, I would agree that there *is* a delicate balance to be considered when it comes to long-term love. Yes, yes, once two people are committed to a life together, sure, bring on the "50/50". (Or whatever works best for you, your man, and your household.) But if it's not worth it to a man to carry the extra load in the beginning of a potential relationship when he's trying to win you over, if he is uninspired to go the extra mile in order to impress you, then forget it. Why bother with him? It's very rare that a man ends up treating a woman better later down the road than he did when she was still just a fantasy to him. If he's playing stingy with you now, he'll play lowlife with you later. So, don't play with *him* at all. You don't need that particular man that bad. I don't know about you, but the quickest way to turn me off is to make me reach for my MasterCard after dinner. And, also for the record, I'd rather be called a gold digger than a damn fool.

Speaking of which . . .

Independent vs. Damn Fool

Are you . . .

• Picking up tabs *and* hailing cabs?

• Changing oil? Washing cars? Pumping gas?

• Pushing your stalled car uphill? Dang, girl. *Chill!*

When a woman is with a man there are just certain things she shouldn't have to do when he's around. The above are a few easy examples of such things. Again, I'm not saying that you should use a man, or try to make him carry a heavier load "just because". I'm saying that there is an *actual* "because". A real, specific "because". Do it because it says to a man (and to yourself) that you are aware of your value, and that you want and value a man who demonstrates that he already sees some of your value, and is, therefore, interested in discovering more about just how truly valuable you are.

A man treating you like a lady, taking you out to dinner, buying you flowers, and covering the costs of a night out with you, says to you *"I'm interested in getting to know you. Thank you so much for spending this time with me. I hope you enjoyed yourself tonight, and I hope that you allow me to take you out again in the immediate future."*

Now, isn't that a beautiful thing? You deserve to experience that kind of chivalry in your life, especially while you're young and single. You're going to be an old woman one day, and perhaps all the bells and whistles won't matter much to you. For now, though, live it up. Soak it up. Savor your youth. Your beauty. Your single years. Make some memories. Some of those memories should be of you being treated like a princess, or queen, at some point in your life. Again, you deserve it. *You. Deserve. It.* You deserve it if you're tall. You deserve it if you're short. You deserve it if you're a size 6. You deserve it if you're a size 26. You deserve it if you own your own home. You deserve it if you have two roommates in a three-bedroom flat. You deserve it because you are a wonderful woman who has much to share with a man who values you. So, do it because it says to a man you know how you deserve to be treated. That you know who you are. You are a woman. *We* are women. And I'm pretty sure men still love that about us.

Sink into your womanhood, your lovely lunar essence. If a man wants to go dollar-for-dollar with you on everything then maybe he should be out on a date with his buddy, Bill, or his best friend, Frank, instead of you. Because if he can't get the *bill*, then quite *frank*ly, you don't need to be out with him. You are not his buddy. You are someone in which he's expressed some level of romantic and sexual interest. Act accordingly. Put your purse up, girl!

Picture This . . .

A woman and man are out on a dinner date. The scampi was fantastic, and the wine, so smooth. The check comes. The man does the *"digging-in-his-back-pocket-for-his-wallet* forward lean", but the woman—quicker than a cowboy in an old Western flick—snatches up her big-dollar bag and whips out her American Express at pretty close to the speed of light.

The guy is thinking he must've dropped his credit card on the floor, and is readying his mouth to thank her for picking it up for him when suddenly she says "I'll get this," and proudly places her gold card inside of the black, vinyl, guest check presenter without even bothering to review the charges, lest she risk looking like she can't afford it.

Oh, my! How impressive am I? she thinks to herself, reading on his face what she believes to be an expression of sincere gratitude and thoughts of just how quickly he can get her to the altar.

In his mind, however, he's thinking . . .

Whoa! This chick is mega macho, and way too desperate for me. He's wondering if she has plans to bend him over the couch later, and whether he'll have a say in the matter. He leans back in his chair and thinks about how long it will take for her to finally get the hint and stop calling him after he's been *"Awfully busy, I'm afraid"* for the remainder of his life.

But I Can Afford to Pay. Why Shouldn't I Show Him That I Can Pull My Weight?

Ok. And why don't you go ahead and sprinkle a little hair on your chest while you're at it. Or better yet, challenge him to a quick arm wrestling match—and *win!*—because it will have a similar effect on the man who was set to impress *you* for the night. One who was all pumped up, confidently-armed, and ready to demonstrate for you some of *his* value. You just cut off his ding-a-ling.

But What If You're Wrong? What If That Makes Him Desire Me Even More?

Well, then, perhaps there's no ding-a-ling for which to be concerned. (At least not one of respectable size. Again, metaphorically speaking, of course.) Moot point. No harm. No foul.

Now, as it applies to the rest of the male population (i.e. those who still have a little something in their boxers worth bragging about) here's something to consider . . .

Your new beau might be a gigolo!

Only a "purse predator" would get all tingly inside over you picking up the check. A normal man won't like you more because you let him off the hook for dinner. He'd sooner be disappointed that you did, because now he has to figure out what his next move can be since you stole his small thunder. He's right where he started credit-wise with you. That's not fair. Let the poor guy treat you. It makes him feel just as good to give as it should make you feel to receive. So, don't just do it for you. Do it for the *both* of you.

Sing Between the Lines

When Beyonce said, "The shoes on my feet -
I bought'em. The house I live in - I bought
it. The rock I'm rockin' - I bought it. 'Cause I
depend on me if I want it." That was some
great stuff. Go Ms. Multi-Millionaire. Always
one to promote Girl Power, she was
schooling us on the self-fulfillment and the
psychological rewards associated with being
able to rely on one's self for the guilty
comforts and pleasures of life we so desire.
That's some sage advice if I've ever heard
some.
However . . .

I'm pretty sure the, now, Mrs. Carter did not
mean for you to interpret this as 'go buy all
of your stuff yourself, and then go hop into
bed and give away your ultimate girly
goodies to some guy who's praying you
won't ask him for Uber fare back home'.
And, as filthy rich as Beyonce is, I'm twice
as sure that Jay-Z picked up the dinner
tabs when he was wooing her into marriage
and motherhood.

Don't be so rich in the pockets that you are dead in the head. Exercise good judgment at any tax bracket.

Don't forget that you are looking for a *quality* man. Not just any old human with a *y* chromosome. Any woman can always, at any time, get "a man". That's occurring every second of the day. You are looking for a man with <u>high quality</u> who demonstrates that he sees the value in you, or, at the least, is optimistic about your potential value so much as to willingly invest in pursuing you. An easy way to demonstrate this is through treating you to a good time when in your company.

A lesser man would just love for us women to foot our own *night-out-with-him* bills, and then come on over to his place to wrap those bill-footing feet right around his no-effort-making neck. Not that there should be a mobile payment device near your nether regions. I certainly don't intend to suggest that you should "prostitute" yourself or demand that a man pay you for sex. What I *am* saying, though, is that everybody with half a brain and who's willing to use that half a brain knows that it's not a good look for a woman to let a man get to the ultimate level of where he is bouncing around inside of her, kissing all on her, and rubbing all over her, when he is not even the slightest bit interested in providing for her in any meaningful way, on even the smallest level. Besides, generosity is an aphrodisiac. (More on that later.)

Still Not Convinced?

Okay. Fast forward thirty years into the future. Your date (the man sitting across from you last night, or—*cringe*—in bed with you this morning) is now married (not to you) with two children. One of these children is an adorable girl who has him wrapped around her finger. She's all grown up now, but Daddy will always see her as his little princess. Let's think about what kind of dating advice Father Dear would give to his little tiara-wearer. What nuggets of wisdom would he share about dating expectations? Got it? You thought about it? Okay. Now think back to all of the things that he may argue against or complain about now *with you* (e.g. having to pick up the dating tabs, sending flowers, putting in the effort, the courting, the helping out, the proving himself worthy, etc.). Would the two expressed dating beliefs match? Probably not. So, it's important for you to understand that "T minus 30 years" *you* are the tiara-wearer. Don't let him play dumb with you. Keep your standards at a respectable height.

If you're not worth the effort to him, then he's not worthy of you.

In Case You Missed It

I can't stress enough that I believe that once two people decide to "do life" together, to marry, and to commit to a solid, lifelong partnership, then, of course, it should become just that: a partnership. I have no qualms with who makes more money, or how household chores are divvied up between a man and a woman. What I am talking about in this book is the courting stages. The part where a man is trying to cast himself in the best light possible in order to get next to the woman that he desires. The part where he is trying to gain access to her wonderful womanly world.

Not The Kind of "Sugar" Adam Levine Was Singing About

If you're just looking for any ol' man to wander through life with, then go for it. Buy his time and attention. Spend away, Miss Moneybags. He'll be all yours.

At least until a richer "Sugar Mama" comes along.

Dating Tip: Know Where to Go

If you're going to be in the dating world it's important that you know what you like or would like to do. Don't be the blind leading the blind. If he has a suggestion, great! If he leaves it up to you, have some ideas of your own. Not sure? Check out the entertainment section of your local newspaper or pull up the Groupon app. Browse the online menus of the nicest restaurants in your area or scroll through a local *food and entertainment* blogger's page. Conduct ten minutes of research to find out where the fun is. Do whatever it is you need to do, but never shrug and say, "Uh . . . I don't know. Wherever's fine." No. Have some thoughts and share them.

Dates are where you go out and play. Have some "playgrounds" in mind. Besides, it's his treat. Remember?

Never Be "In Care Of"

I am not encouraging you to sit back and let a man pay all of your "real life" bills. To be your sole source of livelihood. If you are dating someone and decide to move in with him and you don't have gainful employment, just know that you are at risk of being, eventually, treated like sh*t.

We may get too comfy in a man's mansion (or one-bedroom apartment) and settle into a life of seeing him off to work (while we hit the gym to keep our figures tight, and then the mall to purchase things to show it off) and then greeting him hours later with a *'Welcome home, honey. Don't I look fabulous?'* kiss. But beware. It doesn't take a psychic to predict that he'll eventually assume implied ownership of you, and, thus, have less respect for you.

The man taking total care of you will have less confidence in your ability to take care of yourself as a human being on Planet Earth and, therefore, begin to demonstrate a decreased level of respect for you. When supporting you financially 100% your man will come to feel that he doesn't owe you explanations, or need to consult with you on certain matters, or even consider you at all when making the smallest or biggest of plans. In addition, he'll become more likely to "try you" (i.e. take the bold chance of disrespecting you in some unusual way) when he knows he "pays the cost to be the boss" versus if you were holding your own moneywise.

Never have this stamped on your forehead:

PAID IN FULL

For example, conversations may go like this:
"Yeah, you found another woman's number in my phone. So what?! I pay the bills around here. So, my dear dependent, you can just shut up, stay out of my business, and keep getting taken care of!"
This is what he'll eventually "say" in some way, either through his actions, or in plain English. And it would be pretty pathetic—cry-out-loud sad—if you had to do just that: shut up and take it in order to continue getting taken care of.

Always have your own "cab fare", so to speak. Always have the ability to pack up and hightail it up out of there should a man feel he has purchased the right to mistreat you. Always retain your ability to do for yourself should the man in your life decide to pull a fast one and show you his rump in some unsightly way.

Never become too dependent on a man. Never really *need* him. Keep your résumé fresh, your bank account stacked, your beauty intact, and, therefore, your options open. Your dignity and self-respect look way better on you than any designer dress or shoes his money can buy. Never tolerate any type of disrespect or demeaning treatment, regardless of who's paying the mortgage. I don't care if he has a huge house with 10,000 square feet of luxury living space. *'F'* that square footage. *'F'* those throw pillows. *'F'* that art on the walls. Never trade square footage for a foot up your ass. Be "In Company Of", not "In Care Of", and retain your freedom and ability to flee from a failed or failing relationship.

#2

Stop Texting Him . . .
And Being

Flattered When He

Finally Texts You Back

Thumbs Making You Dumb?

A guy's thumbs can make you think you've really got something special going on with him. Don't fall in love with these faux phalanges. You deserve some real intimacy when it comes to your communication.

Let's be honest. How easy is it for a guy to roll over, reach (possibly past another woman's sleeping body) for his cell phone that's always there anyway, and thumb in "just thinking about you, babe", insert some stupid emoji, and then press *Send* arrow? It's practically effortless. Lazy, even. I'm talking bare-minimum, bottom line lazy. And based on your reply he feels like he's gotten credit for "checking in" or "touching base" with you for the day—or worse, *week*. Then when he finally asks you out, (or *in*, or *over*, more realistically speaking) you feel like the two of you have been working on this wonderful relationship "for like *everrrr*!" This belief, in turn, speeds up the panty-dropping process exponentially.

Because, in your mind, the two of you have been "seeing each other" for a while now. Right?

Uh . . . wrong. No. You, literally, have not been seeing each other. You haven't even been *talking* to each other, my *Homo sapien* sister. You've merely been exchanging digital data—not dating. You've fallen for computer-generated messages on your phone—not him. And quadruple goes for him having not fallen for you. So not only does he not take you out for coffee and a croissant in order to get to know you, he doesn't even have to *call* you, or *speak* to you at all, for that matter. Do you even know the sound of each other's voices without club speakers blaring in the background?

Sadly, rather than enhancing communication between two people, text messages have replaced the basic human-to-human communication required to develop anything even remotely resembling a relationship. A man can just text-a-lover these days. In fact, he can have multiple *textlationships* going, engaging in low-quality courtship—*virtual* courtship—until all land him some real-life sex!

Answer this question: If he didn't have unlimited data how often would you "communicate" with your *beau*friend?

Never be a man's go-to person to "kill some time", or "play naughty" with (i.e. sexting).

Rid yourself of this time-waster. He's not interested in you. He's just bored with himself.

Are You Dating or Data-ing?

Is the only commitment he's involved in with his cell service provider? Is his signal weak and usage time low when it comes to you? Check out the table below to find out.

Dating Plans vs. Data Plans

Dating Plans	Data Plans
He calls or texts you asking if you would like to go out with him this upcoming weekend	He texts you and tells you all about the big fun he had this *past* weekend—without you
He calls you midweek to see if the two of you are still on for your date	He texts you at midnight wanting to know if he can come over "and chill"
He texts you asking if you like Indian cuisine	He texts you asking if you're into Kama Sutra
He takes a quick break after his business meeting to return your call	He returns your calls or texts only during those times he knows that you're guaranteed to be unavailable
He says he wants you to meet his mother	He tells you to call him Daddy

If his favorite love song is *If Texting You Is Wrong, I Don't Wanna Be Right,* then you're not dating him. You're dating his phone.

He's Got Thumb Appeal

Why, look at those little chubbie-wubbies go! All curled and pecking away. Those opposable little devils sure are busy. They look as if they are scoring some major points on his "Rated E for Entertainment" video game. He must be on a super-high level. Oh, wait! —He paused the game. He put down the game controller. That's a cell phone in his hand. Oh, he's texting *you.*

There it is! Your phone just lit up. You see his name.

Sam.

You smile like the Alice in Wonderland cat, then quickly unlock your home screen with your thumbprint to view the message. Let's see what it says . . .

Sam: hey. whatcha doin'?

You think, *Yes!!!!! Let the marathon texting session begin! Conversation ON!!!*

You do some quick thumb exercises to warm up for what you believe will be one of the highlights of your entire day.

You reply.

You: Nothin much. What are you doing? How was practice?

You can't wait to text back in a hurry to show Sam just how attentive to him you are. He's special. And you want to show him that. Oh— there goes the three dots. You smile at Sam's dancing ellipses.

Sam: . . .

Then, here it goes.

Sam: it was ok

Huh? What was ok?—Oh, yeah. 'Practice', you remember.

You wait a few more seconds, hoping to see those dancing ellipses again. Hoping he's got something to add to that bland, three-word reply. The all lowercase font and missing period stung a little, too. It seems half-hearted. It kind of says something. He keeps hitting you with the *lazy lowercase*. You try not to read into too much, but something inside of you begs the question: Am I not worth a Shift key?

You shake off those critical thoughts, giving Sam the benefit of the doubt. Besides, his next text will clear things up. You just know it will. But those ellipses don't come as soon as you hope. As quickly as they did last time.

You, wanting to keep the "conversation" in motion, text the following:

You: That's nice. I bet you did great. Your teammates are so lucky to have you. You should totally be captain. You guys would be unstoppable if you were.

You hit *Send* and wait.

And wait . . .

And wait . . .

It feels like an eternity, but in actuality it's only been about 5 seconds.

Six.

Seven.

Eight.

In that space of eight seconds your heart sinks a little bit as you wonder what happened. Where did Sam go? Where are those damn ellipses?!!

Maybe something distracted him, you think. *Damn distraction!* Did he suddenly feel a gnat on his leg and had to smack it? Was he outside floating atop an inflated flamingo in his community pool and topple over, dropping his phone into the water? Did another call or text come in right at the very moment that he prepared to respond to your last comment? Did someone knock on his door? Was it the FBI? Oh my gosh! Are they raiding his house? Have the feds funkied up your day? Did the real Men-in-Black just hijack your hustle?! *Where are you, Sam????!!!!!* You want to scream at the phone.

You scroll up a tad to re-read the message thread. To review the conversation, brief as it was, to see if you missed something, or if that awful autocorrect feature you keep forgetting to disable left Sam suspended in confusion on the other end, trying to decipher your unintentional riddle. Then you wonder if maybe you simply said something wrong. Something weird. Inappropriate. You read the thread a third time, this time paying special attention to *your* last text:

You: That's nice. I bet you did great. Your teammates are so lucky to have you. You should totally be captain. You guys would be unstoppable if you were.

An embarrassed chill drizzles upon you. Your heart skips a funny little beat as you scrutinize your message that, now, seems totally weird. You analyze his previous reply, the one just preceding that message, and wonder if you can read something in his tone. In those three words. You can't tell. So, you go back to your last message again. Did you say too much? Did you offend him? Did you bring up a sensitive topic?

Oh, man! I shouldn't have brought up the captain thing. That may be a sore subject for him. He must be mad at me. Is he? Oh, no. I've gotta find out for sure. I have to know.

But instead of asking "are you mad at me?" — which would make you look super stupid with a little paranoid on top—you decide to send this instead:

You: Oh, man! I just scheduled my appointment to take my MCAT. Can' t wait to be done with this dumb test. #MDgoals, #doctorhurtles, #sleepwanted

You want to sound smart. Ambitious. Busy. Humble. You hope he sees all these qualities in you by reading this new and improved text.

You wait.

No ellipses.

No reply.

You hurry up and follow up with:

You: Do you think your roommate still has his study guide? I could really use the savings (insert 'blowing bangs' emoji).

Nice move, you think, mentally patting yourself on the back. You see, the text before this one was only a statement. Something that didn't necessarily require a response, per say. But a question, you think. A *question* requires an answer. You tell yourself, *He'll have to respond this time.*

Unless he's mad.

You continue to wait.

And wait . . .

And wait . . .

Five whole minutes pass when you decide to text your friend, Anna, just to make sure your messaging app didn't suddenly stop functioning.

You: Hey girl

Anna: Hey! Whatsup?

You: Not much. Just wanted to say Hi and see how you were.

At this point you really don't give a damn how Anna's doing because, at this moment, you've just confirmed that your messaging app is working just fine, and, therefore, you're feeling even more panicked and paranoid about Sam's digital disappearance. Adding insult to injury, not only is your phone functioning like it's fresh out of the box, you've got all four bars. Anna's reply came on the absolute heels of your text to her. Almost as quick as yours did for Sam.

Anna is in the middle of replying, but *her* dancing ellipses simply annoy you as you now silently rush her along from your couch. *"Hurry up, girl. Say what you gotta say, already!"* you mumble at Anna's ellipses, wishing they were Sam's instead.

Anna is still typing away.

Ugh! You click the home button just to make it stop.

You begin thinking about Sam again. Where did he go so fast? What happened within those terribly short eight seconds that totally caused him to ghost you?

Oh, wait! —Your screen lights up again.

Dammit! It's Anna.

You take your silent frustrations out on her.

My goodness! Doesn't she have anything better to do? It's Saturday for Pete's sake! I just wanted to say Hi. What's with all the ping-ponging? She seriously needs to get a life! I mean, I like her, but geesh!

You choose to ignore Anna. You'll get with her later. Right now you have some sulking, analyzing, dissecting, scenario-painting, and then more sulking to do. Making it your mission to work out in your mind exactly why Sam went *i-AWOL*, you lie back on your bed and stare at the ceiling fan.

Meanwhile . . .

On the other side of the city, Sam, who thought he'd just check in with you for the day, and already has you calendared for a tentative "coochie cash-in" next Friday, is now back to playing his video game. He's not yet brushed his teeth, and he just passed gas for the thousandth time today. He, too, is a little frustrated himself because thirty minutes ago he texted this beautiful girl he met last night, and she hasn't replied. *Petra*, she said her name was. He wonders if that was a fake name he'd been given. An alias. He suspected that she might not actually call when she appeared to be, if only, tolerant of him when he practically hacked his number into her phone. Her aloofness was sexy, though. He loves a woman who is just too busy for him. It's his weakness. His kryptonite.

Sam especially liked it when he waved *Bye* to Petra again in the parking lot and she didn't wave back as she climbed into her silver 'Stang with the personalized tag that read: KP1T MVN. *She's just so preoccupied,* he thinks. It drives him wild. In fact, when he texted you, it was only to kill some time and rebuild some ego. But he got annoyed that you kept texting back. Especially when you texted the stupidest, most butt-kissing content. *Captain*?! *What does* she *know about baseball?* he thought to himself, hip to *your* game. He tells himself he can't stand girls who try too hard. It's such a turnoff. There's no *challenge.* No chase. He's a runner. He likes to—Oops! —There he goes cutting the cheese again.

And right there, in that moment, back on the other side of town, your entire Saturday has just been ruined, and it's only noon. You, now, spend the entire afternoon and evening thinking about what and why you said what you said, and what Sam is doing these very moments instead of texting you back.

You could've saved yourself a lot of heartache and headache by keeping it simple. When he texts "hey", *you* text "hey". And, it doesn't have to be right away. Don't break the sound barrier reaching for your phone to reply to him. Slow down. *Oh, but I don't want to appear rude, like I'm ignoring him,* you say. And to that I say *Get over it.* A delayed text never made any reasonable, *sane* man who is interested in you lose all hope and throw in the towel on you. They wait. (As they should.) They wait for you to respond. And they busy themselves until then.

Simple works. Stick to the basics. Don't say more than what he's saying or ask more than what he's asking. Don't try to draw out the conversation just to be "in communication" with him. If he wants to extend the conversation or talk about something specific, he'll text you. Better yet, he'll CALL you!!!!

Take Those Pants Off And Put Your Bra Back On!

#3

Stop Shopping for Him

Spending Money: The Prequel

Ladies, we've got our purses open again. *Naughty. Naughty.* Only this time, rather than to pay for dinner and dessert, we're spending money *before* the date. We're making prequel purchases.

He calls. Yes, *calls*. He actually hit the little phone icon instead of the envelope.

Blake. He's so freakin' cute. What's that? He asks you out?

O-M-G!!!!!!!!!!!

Ok. You've gotta get ready for this date. After all, he's taking you to the best C-List restaurant in the borough. You instantly start thinking of what you're going to wear.

You go to your closet. You can barely squeeze in with all the fabulous garments you've got hanging, and folded, and stacked. You spend the next thirty minutes hunting for the perfect outfit to spend the evening with Blake—with no success!

What?!

Not one single item can pass the Blake Test in your mind. You've gotta hit the mall. And you've gotta bring your credit card with you.

Ladies, spending hundreds of dollars in one single trip to the mall on clothes and lingerie before a date, all in hopes that he will find you sexy and attractive *before* and *when* you eventually "give up the goods to him" is ridiculous.

Oh, I hope he finds me sexy, you think to yourself as you hold up to your body a triple-digit article of two-dollar fabric, checking yourself out in the tri-fold mirror.

Um, you're a woman. *Of course* he finds you sexy!

(Yes. Read that again.)

You are a woman. Therefore, men do find you sexy and attractive. Yet somehow you forget this. You break the bank all in order to visually seduce him. To entice him into wanting you. Stop going for the hard sell. You are already *beyond* good enough.

Now, don't get me wrong, a little advertisement is healthy and smart. Hair, makeup, tastefully-selected clothing, perfume. Fine. But the over-the-top efforts, the going the extra mile in order to appear attractive is way too much and speaks directly to a woman's self-worth. Her self-esteem.

First of all, if you don't think that the guy you're going out with thinks you're attractive then why are you going out with him? Why be around him? Why are you trying so hard to make this person see "good" in you? Who's wooing who here?

No man is going out to the mall spending hundreds of dollars trying to pick out the perfect outfit for his date with you tonight.

No guy, especially on the first date, is buying several alternate outfits or purchasing new underwear in hopes that a woman will think he is attractive. A man searches his closet (or clothes hamper) picking out something to wear on a date without spending more than five minutes on the task. He's a 5-minute planner. We're 5-hour—5-*day*—planners! Why? Don't forget that we are the prize.

Once you relinquish your position as the prime object of desire (aka "the prize") in the dating dance, then you have set the tone and quality of your "relationship to come" with this man. And a man of lesser quality will gladly have you jump

through hoops and over sky-high hurdles to
sweep him off his man-sized feet.

Think about all the money you've wasted on "You
Know Who" (insert the last guy you went out on a
date with that turned out to be a disappointment).
Think back to that dress you purchased in
anticipation of a night that, unfortunately, just
didn't go at all as you'd hoped. All the hype. All
the hair. All the money spent for a night that only
ended up with you on the phone with your best
girlfriend, telling her what an awful time you had.

No, don't start wishing you'd left the tags on. No
one wants to Salsa in your sweat, or boogie in
your buyer's remorse. No, leave that dress in your
closet as a reminder of your wastefulness when it
comes to all of this bait-buying. Your best lure is
always in the allure of being a woman.

Self-Confidence Is Free

I want to let you in on a little secret. There are
women—right now—walking this water-covered
rock we call home, maybe even the same ones
that you think may envy you for your beauty or
career, etc., that are not spending a single dime

on prepping for some "Uncertain". They are being themselves. Dressing comfortably. Wearing what's already in their closets. They're not banging their heads against the wall thinking about what he may be thinking about them, and they are getting pretty great guys. Not because they are better than you, but because they are better to themselves than you are to yourself. Because they are better at *being* themselves than you are at being you. They are shrewder, more practical, logical, or maybe just downright cheap, but it's working for them. It's working for her. You must consider if what you're doing is working for you. If it isn't, switch it up. Know that you are good enough just the way you are and with exactly what you already have.

Moral of the Story

Don't you wish you could get back all the time and money, all the energy that you invested in trying to appeal to a man you barely knew. One you only "dealt with" for a few weeks. Even just the money you spent on shaving cream, in hindsight, seems like a bad investment. Disappointment makes it appear as if it was all for nothing. But while it didn't yield the results you intended that duddy date doesn't have to be a total loss because you can gain *"know better"*. You've lived, now learn. When you change your mind and your actions you end up changing your life. So, as it turns out, *Whatshisname* wasn't as worthless as you thought.

Challenge: Part I

Look through your panty drawer. Go ahead. Open it up. Let's take a walk down memory lane. (I'll give you time to get there. Ready? Okay.) Those, over there, the pink polka-dotted pair, for whom did you buy that pair? Can you remember? If so, how did he turn out? Overall and in detail, please. How exactly did things work out with him? Where and with whom is he now?

What about those? The red ones. Ring a bell? Bring back any memories? Did they result in long-term love, or short-term good times? Was it worth it? What about sexually? Did you even receive any reciprocal sexual satisfaction? You know, the kind that he made sure he got from you before the two of you parted ways for the night.

This is not a recollection of shame. It is an exercise simply meant to open your eyes to the ways in which you inappropriately invest in men, and to challenge you to consider changing your methodology. Don't waste the embarrassment you may feel right now. Feel it. Really feel it. Close your eyes and roll around in it. Get it all on you. Make a mental note of how it feels, and why.

Challenge: Part II

Throw out all of your panties. Yes, you read that right. Throw them out and start fresh. Get yourself some new undies. And think twice before you buy (for someone else) again. Don't be deterred by the cost of replacement. You can restock for about a hundred bucks. (Okay. Maybe not luxury lingerie, but why would you need that right now if you are single and planning to keep your clothes on for the right person next time?) Catch a sale and get yourself about twenty new pair. Then make a commitment to yourself that no man who wouldn't sacrifice for you—do for you when things gets serious—will ever get to see, touch, smell, or take off those panties of yours.

Take Those Pants Off And Put Your Bra Back On!

#4

Stop Telling Him He's Cute

Going Compliment Crazy

Cute guys have small penises. Fact or Fiction?

Okay. Fiction. But humor me.

Imagine if for every compliment you give a man on his looks you take a centimeter off his penis length—and *two* off its girth!

"*Nooooooooo!!!!!!*" you scream in slow motion like your new-version phone is free-falling its way into a rest stop toilet.

Ok, now let's use this penis-size-reduction scenario as a metaphor for a man's level of interest in you after you've complimented him to *ad nauseam*. A measure of his desire to make you <u>Mrs</u>. Excuse Me, But My Penis is Getting Smaller by The Compliment.

Picture the manliest man from the silver screen.
Yes, the old movies of your great grandma's era.
The man that had your great grandma thinking
thoughts that you don't even want to *think* about
her thinking right now. John Wayne, for
example—The Duke, as he was called—didn't
have women running around talking about how
pretty his eyes were, or how cute of a smile he
had. Harrison Ford (your grandma's crush and
the OG version of whomever you consider the
hottest male movie star of today) didn't have the
ladies going on and on about how awesome his
hair looked, or how adorable he looked in his
chaps. It's unnatural. Awkward. And it won't
score you any points. By the contrary, it may
actually cause you to lose points with him. He'd
rather be the one giving the compliments. Keep
him in his comfort zone. Lay off his looks already.

Gassing Him Up Will Drive Him Away—From *You* . . . and to Another Woman's House to Pick Her Up For Their Date

Stop inappropriately complimenting these men!
Quit telling a guy he's cute, or hot, or sexy. Unless
he is already your husband, you must stop doing
this. It's just not attractive, or effective.

Think about it. Who does a guy pursue? Who does
he go after and, ultimately, end up with? Is it the
girl who is buttering him up with compliments on
his Justin-Bieber-inspired bang? Or is it the
woman who ignores his '*do* and, instead, focuses

on his "*does*", as in what he *does* to show her some love and consideration?

If you said the woman who's tweeting about his lovely locks, you're wrong. By the contrary, it's the woman who didn't step out of character and start chasing him around the city that wins his heart; the one who *he* feels compelled to compliment.

He can't chase you if you're already chasing him.

We must stop putting men on pedestals, chasing them and wooing them. It's not attractive to them. While guys may seem to enjoy the attention and compliments, while their egos may love that we show obvious signs that we want them, it does not make them want *us* in return. It just doesn't. Don't waste your breath, or your time.

Sad Scenario

Her: "You look so good tonight, Mike. I just love that shirt on you. And your gauges are *suh-weet!*"

Him: "Awww. Thanks, Sarah."

Her: "It's Suzie."

Him: "Oh, yeah. Sorry. Thanks, Suzie. That's really nice of you to say."

His <u>Mind</u>: *Now who is that over there ignoring me? So sexy!*

Him: Uh. Would you excuse me, Sandra?"

His <u>Feet</u>: (*Walking away from "Suzie" and toward "Ms. Minding Her Own Business and Doesn't Give a Damn About His Shirt".*)

So, Who Does a Man Chase?

Not the chaser, that's for sure! Not the groupie. Not the girl who has been trying so hard to impress him, to prove her worth. He chooses the woman who is naturally confident and makes him chase *her* for any of her attention.

If It'll Just *Kill* You To Not Pay Him A Compliment

If you absolutely *must* compliment a man, compliment him the right way. Compliment him on things that actually matter. Things that he's done, specifically for *you* in his efforts to court you.

For example, if a man takes you to a wonderful restaurant, compliment him on his selection of such a fine eatery. Tell him what wonderful taste in restaurants he has. What a wonderful dining experience he has planned for the two of you to enjoy together. Pay him a genuine compliment on his exceptional taste that just so happens to complement yours.

Another meaningful compliment could involve a suggestion, or referral he may have provided you with. Say, for example, you were leaving for a business trip or a vacation and he was able to recommend a certain "must visit" venue, or an unforgettable sight for you to take in. Perhaps he recommended a hotel that has the best on-site spa services that your size sevens have ever felt. Or maybe he gave you a great tip about how to clean your dog, *Poncho's*, fangs! You get the point.

Ditch the low-grade heinie-kissing kudos and limit your compliments to only those things that involve his efforts to make you happy and *his*.

Compliment his efforts, not his earrings.

Acceptable Exceptions To Complimenting A Man on His Looks

You may say to him . . .

Your body looks amazing! - If he lost 150 pounds since he last updated his datemedarling.com profile picture, and you were pleasantly surprised.

Your eyes look fantastic! - If the two black eyes he received a couple weeks ago defending your honor at a shady bar finally faded.

You have the best smile! - If the front tooth he got knocked out in the same bar fight has been replaced by a beautiful, porcelain crown.

Take Those Pants Off And Put Your Bra Back On!

#5

Stop Competing for Him

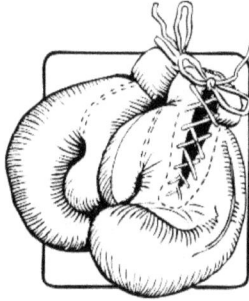

Brute Ain't Cute

No, Honey. Those aren't the kind of "dukes" he wanted to see you with.

It's always excruciatingly embarrassing to see two or more women on a talk show, or some Reality Show Reunion, fighting over a guy who is sitting on the stage smirking about it all. I should note that it is also very rare that the man for whom they'd kill is anyone who could even remotely be considered a catch by anyone besides those particular women. Rarely are they good-looking. Rarely are they rich. Very rarely are they educated. And "rarely on *'roids"* are they good to either one of the women.

So, if women are fighting over the likes of *these* men just imagine the battles that take place—the wars that are waged—over men with a mere morsel of value or, Heaven forbid, of decent-to-high quality.

Dueling for Him

Regardless of a man's quality quotient it is never a good idea for a woman to fight, or even argue with another woman, over him. And while, certainly, coming to blows over a guy is approaching the extreme, it is not the only wacky way in which we fight for "He We Think Is Ours". And by "fighting" I mean *competing*.

Think you're not fighting for him because you don't have your dukes up? Think again. Here are some other ways you may be, or may have, fought (aka "competed") for a man:

- comparing yourself with, and trying to outdo, other women in his life

- hating on other women, or being catty over him

- putting on a show for others when you're with him (e.g. squeezing his hand extra tight when another woman crosses your path)

- criticizing his new, or current girlfriend/wife

- betraying your own gender with the tired, old, sell out statement: *"I'm not like most girls/women."*

- making your home a hideout for a deadbeat dad

• fighting his battles for him, or *with* him, even when you know he's dead wrong

How have you been competing? What's been your competition style? Think about it, and then discontinue it. The truth is, we as women never have to compete for the man who is really right for us.

The aforementioned are some less-extreme ways in which we compete for a man. The next two ways are at the more extreme end of things and should be avoided at all costs.

#1 - Ho'ing Around: There's Something About *Married*

Ho'ing around is a major way in which we sometimes compete for a man. But first, allow me to clarify. As used in this book, a *ho* (not to be confused with *whore*) isn't a woman who enjoys sex. A ho is not a woman who feels free to succumb to her sexual urges. Who sleeps around, etc. A ho, as I use it in this book, is short for *ho*mewrecker.

Sometimes we temp. Other times we put in full time hours. But in either case, we are never provided with any insurance. Many of us may find this kind of work too demeaning to do altogether and pass on such a gig. (Good job, by the way, because it can happen to even the best of us in an emotionally-weak chapter of our lives.)

No matter how you arrived at such a point in your life, it is essential to your well-being that you recognize that you are dead-ass wrong (That's really, *really* wrong.) for giving your good loving to a lowlife cheater with absolutely no intention of leaving his wife, three children, two dogs and frog—which he *shouldn't,* by the way, since that would make him kin to The Devil. Just saying.

Before you take another call from Satan's sibling, take this 60-second quiz to find out where you rank on the '*ho*rometer'.

The Comprehensive Ho Assessment

1) Do men who are unavailable seem to appeal to you more than those who are single? Is *There Something About* Married???

2) Would the same man you turned down last month have had a better chance at being with you if he wore a wedding ring?

3) Do you suddenly liven up in the company of other women's men, even if they aren't particularly attractive?

4) Does your voice get higher? Do you blink three times as much? Does your chest, coincidentally, seem to poke out further than it has all day when around your friend's man?

If you answered *Yes* to 1 or more of the above questions you need to submit your letter of resignation and start a new romantic path right away because you are, indeed, a *Ho*mewrecker.

*Ho*mewrecking is not a smart path to be on as it will only leave the following in its wake:

✓ pain

✓ tears

✓ humiliation

✓ guilt

✓ regret

✓ ridicule

✓ embarrassment

✓ hate

✓ paranoia

✓ bitterness

✓thoughts of vengeance

✓bad karma

If you were a first-time offender don't beat yourself up too bad over your slip in judgment because, as you just read, karma will address this with you one day, usually when you least expect it. (Sorry. But the karmic ass-kicking is definitely queued up and coming). So instead of guilting yourself to death while you await this spiritual spanking, why not resolve to treating yourself better, and to treating your fellow woman better. This goes triple for repeat offenders.

Relationships can be challenging enough without us tipping around with each other's men. We all deserve better. We must battle against selling ourselves short. When we inject ourselves into someone else's relationship we can cause a lot of hurt. We can cause emotional injury to ourselves, to him, to his wife, to his children, and, depending on the outcome of such a clandestine affair, even to our *own* families. What's more, being someone's sidepiece is beneath us all. And not only is *ho*'ing hazardous to your mental, emotional, and psychological health, depending on how "passionate" (aka *crazy*) the legitimate woman is about her man and their relationship, it could even end up being hazardous to your being alive.

#2 - Criminal-Minded Madness

I don't want to spend a lot of time on this, but as I'd just alluded to, sometimes a person's passion can result in some serious tragedy for one or all parties involved in a particular relationship, or love triangle. You really don't want to fall among the statistics of women in prison, on death row, or already dead because of some relationship they just couldn't resist or let go of. *Let it go* are three of the most underappreciated, unobeyed words in modern human history. Though often hard to execute (no pun intended), they are the most important words following a break up, or other type of rejection. If we are to move on, this would be Step One.

Aggression may also be expressed on a much smaller scale. It may take on the form of threats, or trash-talking. The hypothetical scenarios we tell to others that begin with *"If she . . ."* and end with *"I'm going to . . . "* are examples of competing with another woman in a dangerously unhealthy way. Let's stop all of this. We mustn't let our emotions get us into trouble. Reality Shows may have us thinking that threatening to physically harm someone is normal and acceptable, but it's not. Just watch Oxygen's *Snapped* to get an idea of the kind of fate that awaits a woman who just couldn't let it go, or who thought she could get

away with getting another woman *out* of the way.
You'll find no happy endings.

Stay Strapped

A good soldier always stays strapped. He or she never enters into combat without the proper weaponry on either his or her hip, or around his or her waist or shoulder. Likewise, a smart woman stays strapped. Her weaponry is always around her shoulders. It's her bra. She keeps her bra on, meaning she never leaves home without her dignity and integrity. She stays strapped in the healthiest way.

Snapless Broads Unite

Before He Cheats is a helluva catchy song. I sing along to it myself when I hear it playing over retail store speakers, lip-syncing perfectly on cue as if I were Carrie Underwood herself.

However, Carrie didn't sing about the likely aftermath of such a revenge-filled rampage. She skipped the part about the arraignment, and subsequent trial and sentencing. You see, Ms. Underwood didn't take into consideration that some of us won't want to stop at busting up his truck, but, instead, have the irresistible urge to take the bat to him next. Some ladies may want to turn that Louisville Slugger into a Louisville Slug-*Him!*, forgetting that even the hottest chick ends up looking like a busted broad once she's in the penal system. Why even flirt with violence this way? Don't let penis land you in The Pen. Again, watch Oxygen's *Snapped* or *Women Behind Bars* to get a preview of your life (or the end of it) should you be tempted to go the retaliatory route and take things fatally too far. He ain't worth it. Dead or alive.

Don't you dare snap! Keeping yourself together is your job—your obligation—regardless of someone else's actions or choices. Stay strapped, not snapped!

In addition to potentially landing us in big trouble, competing with another woman for a man is truly a fruitless endeavor. A frustrating waste of time and energy. Because, usually, when we do this, we're competing with other women in ways that won't win us the war. And we're fighting with the wrong weapons.

Bringing a Butt to a Boob Fight

Don't be presumptuous, ladies. Don't be fooled by your "hungry-hungry ego". A man's compliments of you can give you a false sense of both comfort and superiority. Just because a man constantly compliments you on your big behind, for example, does not mean he won't be *extremely* attracted to someone who has very little to show for in the buttocks department. Just because the guy you like, or the guy "you're with" is always talking about how nice your double-Cs are does not, in any way, under any circumstances, mean that he won't leave you and your "carbon copies" for a AA-Cup Wonder. Nor does it mean that because he often tells you he could get lost in your ocean-blue eyes that the next brown-eyed babe who walks into the room won't give him whiplash. You see, the things that you believe are his *exclusives*, his *non-negotiables* or "requirements" of a woman, may only just apply to you.

Time and time again women are shocked to find out that their man is messing around with someone that they (themselves) perceive to be not on her level. "*She doesn't even have a butt! My man likes something to hold onto at night.*" Or "*Her face looks weird.*" Or "*She's fat.*" Etcetera. Etcetera. Criticisms like these will find you looking quite foolish in the end when you see your man on a news feed with someone who you, mistakenly, thought you were superior to in his eyes. Because the real fact of the matter is . . .

Men like women.

They like all different kinds of women. They like different things about *different* women. Perhaps your long hair or full hips are what he most appreciates on *you*. But Sharon's long legs and small little backside coupled with her beautiful big eyes are what he most appreciates on *her*. And maybe her attributes on her trump your attributes on you—to *him*.

It's the luck of the draw, ladies. So, here's the remedy for all this mistaken sense of superiority. Understand that men can appreciate, and most certainly do, a variety of different qualities on a variety of different women. Don't assume that his passion comes in one flavor, or that his desires are under your sole proprietorship. Don't deduce in error that because he likes chocolate ice cream it must mean he doesn't like vanilla cupcakes. He likes it all. *They* like it all.

The truth is you don't know what dynamic is in operation when it comes to a man's attraction to someone else that you, in your mind, consider to be not "his type". The tall, lanky girl he's looking at may remind him of someone from his past that he still holds dear. The short, plus-sized girl's laugh may be warm and contagious in a silly and fun way, and he finds this just the kind of giggle therapy he needs after a hard day at work.

A particular woman may have both obvious *and* hidden qualities that the man you enjoy *enjoys*. That's not to take away from you, however. You are still the same beautiful queen that you've always been. So don't start looking in the mirror scrutinizing yourself once you find out about his vanilla cupcake stash. Don't go running to *Dr. Plumpitup* to get those lips injected. Because it's not about what you're not. It's simply about what he happens to be attracted to at a particular moment in time. (Like while he's standing at Gas Pump 3, eating his dollar burrito, and a woman walks by with her "woman parts" with her and all, and suddenly she's the one he's been waiting for all his life . . . at least until the lady in the Lexus drives up to Gas Pump 4.)

You just can't predict what a man will do, or who may catch his eye the moment you take yours off him. So, what the heck? Drop competition from your romantic toolbox and pick up some unwavering self-esteem.

Beware of BEGOS

Your eye may not pop out of its socket and dangle by its optic nerve. And your teeth may not rot and assemble themselves in binary code fashion but, like any other zombie, you'll definitely run low on gray matter when you suffer from this self-esteem-lowering syndrome.

BEGOS (Bruised Ego Syndrome) can turn you into an illogical, unreasonable, obsessive, competitive, bad-decision-making monster! Sometimes when you're rejected by a man—unexpectedly so—you can become jealous of anything with a pulse and would want to fight a ninety-year-old lady if the man who just dumped you looked at her twice. Or, in the case that he begins dating someone else, your replacement can look like an extra-terrestrial, but through your BEGOS-afflicted, distorted vision, she's giving every supermodel a run for their money. And you hate her.

BEGOS can have you begging back Quasimodo or begging for the return of lost attention from a man that your reasonable mind knows is ridiculously unworthy of you. The unexpected rejection mutates the "Sanity DNA" in your brain. You could've been secretly plotting how to get rid of this subpar person, but he beat you to the punch, or lost interest in you, or perhaps another woman has "entered stage left" and, suddenly, this gross, rude, soul-less, lying, cheating, intellectually impaired—lacking in all things loveable—miserable chunk of mass becomes Idris Elba meets The Dalai Lama meets Nikola Tesla meets Superman. Don't let this Man of "Steal" rob you of your joy, dignity, or decency. He's the same old dirtbag you didn't want in the first place. Be glad that his ass is gone and let E.T. have'em!

#6
Stop Blocking His Shots

"Why, Of Course, You Can Get The Door for Me."

One of the best ways we women can put our bras back on is for us to sit back and allow a man to work his manly magic and perform his gentlemanly deeds. Stop disallowing a man to be a gentleman. L*et* him open doors. Let him pull out your chair. Let him buy you flowers and candy. Put your chests back in, ladies. Stop trying to prove your independence and ability to "hold it down" so bad that you wind up with a 35-year-old dependent you didn't give birth to. Don't get all defensive like it's an insult for a man to want to open up some heavy oak for you. And don't try to do it better than he can. He knows you can open up a door without breaking a nail. You do it all day long without him. But it's called *being nice*. Being a gentleman. Calm down and soften up.

If a man wanted to be out with his masculine idol he'd take out the Dos Equis dude.

Think about a confident woman who gets everything she wants from a man. Is she the one putting in the initial effort? Is she pulling out her own chair and yanking open her own doors when in his company? Nope. She just sits back and lets the man do what he, innately, loves to do. She would bring out the lower male in a man if she denied him these opportunities to flex his pursuer muscles. And we never want to summon such a creature.

Cool Chick, Fool Chick

Who told us that guys like girls who don't like men to make a fuss over them? Who spread *that* lie? What madman went around manipulating womankind with that rotten package of bologna?! I believe this sparked the beginning of what I call The *Cool Chick, Fool Chick* Phase.

During the *Cool Chick, Fool Chick* Phase some women begin to believe that being low maintenance, or "more chill" when dealing with a man is the way to go. They pass on nights out and settle instead for nights in . . . doing the same things that they could have (or had just done) by themselves in their own homes, thinking that this would instantly make them more desirable to "the menzez".

Do any of these statements sound familiar?

Oh, I don't mind just hanging out at your apartment tonight. Dressed up? Who, me? Oh, no. I always wear sequins to watch Netflix.

Sure, we can hang out at my place. Let me order some takeout. No, don't worry about it. I got it. Oh, hang on a sec.— 'Yes, this will be delivery'—You like meat lovers?

No, I don't mind if you and your friends come over and raid my fridge. Eat up, boys!

Oh, you shouldn't have wasted your money on flowers just for me. Just seeing you is treat enough.

Oh, don't worry about driving me. I don't mind taking two buses, a bike, and an Uber to get back home from a night spent with you. That will just give me more idle time to think of you . . . and us.

No, take my car. You are your friends should ride in style. Here—don't forget my gas card. It's unlimited.

This is in no way "being cool". This is simply being very, very *unsmart*. (Yes, I'm making up more words.) This brainless behavior won't land you a quality man. It will only land you in the Regret Ward when it finally dawns on you that you practically begged a guy to use and take advantage of you. Off your knees! *Immediately!*

Yes, He Should Have

When a guy does wonderful things for you such as pulling out your chair, opening your car door, sending you flowers and sweet treats, you should refrain from saying *"Aww, you* shouldn't *have."*

What?!! Yes. He *should* have. And more importantly, he *did.*

Resist the urge to say, *"You didn't have to do that."*

Um . . . He knows that!

He knows he didn't have to buy you flowers. But he did. He *chose* to do so in order to make you smile, feel special, or to encourage you to thank him with a hug, or a kiss on the cheek.

When he does these nice things for you and you tell him that he didn't have to, do you really want him thinking *"Oh, I didn't?"* Or, *"What?! These long stems don't score me any points?"* Or, worse, *"Oh, so you're easy? Damn. I wish I would've known that before I spent the fifty bucks. Now you tell me!"*

Now, do you want him thinking any of those things after he's done something nice for you? Of course not.

And while we're on the subject, let me introduce you to two very powerful words:

Thank. You.

As stated, no man wants to hear that he didn't have to or shouldn't have bought you something. So stop saying it, thinking that it makes you sound easy-breezy and low maintenance. Instead, substitute those self-starving words with the words *Thank You.* Yes. Just thank the man and mean it.

The same goes for rejecting his compliments of you. Refrain from voiding out the compliments he pays you by saying something negative about yourself.

Him: Your hair looks great tonight.

You: Oh, no. I need to get my ends trimmed. They're horrible.

Um, why are you saying this? Especially when you know good and well that if he said, *"Oh, yeah? Let me get a better look"* and proceeded to grab a swatch of your frayed locks for closer examination, and then agreed with you, you'd feel pretty bad.

Never draw a man's attention to something you don't like about yourself. Never.

But, maybe you're saying this to let him know that it gets even better. That if he thinks you look great now, just wait until he sees you with your hair actually salon fresh. Nice try. But this is unnecessary. Just say *Thank You.*

Let Him Show You His G-Spot, Then You Show Him Yours

Forget oysters. *Generosity* is the ultimate aphrodisiac. How many times have you fallen for a guy who has treated you like a queen? He doesn't even have to be good-looking, just "good to *you*". And that's the best kind of good that a man can be.

What a fantastic thing it is to be treated with kindness and tenderness. To be treated like you really matter. A man who is generous to me holds a special place in my heart. I love when a man shows me his G-Spot, his *Generosity-Spot*. It makes me want to really tune in to who he is and what we could be. Generous men are the most attractive men because they are the men who aren't afraid to shower a woman with a little pampering in order to gain her favor. Give these men the props they deserve. How do you do that? You show them *your* G-Spot, in this case your *Gratitude-Spot*. Be grateful for the kindness and generosity he shows you by saying, you guessed it, *Thank You*—and meaning it!

Just So We're Clear: The words *Thank You* are not to be substituted with hot, bed-burning sex. You thank a man with your words, not your womanly parts.

Consideration: Generosity's First Cousin

If Bob doesn't help you with jack, then maybe you should leave Bob <u>for</u> Jack.

1988. *Control* album.

Janet asked it best:

*What have you done for me
lately?
Ooooh . . . Ooooh. . . Ooooh.
Yeah!!!*

Okay, let's consider some things:

The man on your mind, can he change the oil in a car like an automotive technician? *Yes???* He changes his *own* oil, you say? *Cool!*

Does he ever offer to change the oil in *your* car? Does he pop the hood of your Honda and get at that dipstick every once in a blue moon?

Does he notice that your car is making a deafening screeching sound that's totally familiar to him, and then ask you about it? Or does he pretend like he doesn't hear it at all, even as it's making the hair stand up on the back of his neck?

Does he pretend he doesn't see your rear tire wobbling on the verge of falling off as you drive away from his place, just mere moments after giving him mind-blowing whoopee? Or is he too busy exhaling with relief that you finally left?

Seriously, let's take a mental tally of his basic consideration toward you. When he comes by your place and happens to see (as he's using your john) that your bathroom faucet is dripping, does he ask you if you have a wrench laying around, and then put in some wristwork? Does he grab the gigantic garbage bag sitting by the door and toss it into the dumpster for you on his way out of your apartment? Is he that irresistibly-considerate? If he is, keep'em! If he isn't dump him along with the bulky bag.

Here's another example to get you thinking about what it means to be considerate. When you agree to meet the man on your mind at 11:00 pm at the corner coffee shop for a little late-night, last-minute Calculus study session, does he come back from the barista's counter with *two* cups of warm, caffeinated deliciousness? Or does he sip his lone skinny latte in front of you, wearing a Juan Valdez hat, asking if you can go over derivatives one more time?

You know what? Forget these examples. Does he think about you in considerate ways *at all?*

Think about your friends. Your family. These are people who have a genuine concern for you, and who find it natural to want to help you with the things that they are able to, and comfort you in the ways that they can. It's not using. It's friendship. It's relationships. It's consideration. It's *normal.*

Give Him a Workout

Exercising muscles help to build them up and make them healthier. The more you use a muscle, the stronger it becomes. Let a man exercise his heart muscle, his "helpful muscles" when he deals with you, not the one that shrinks back down to size once he's done with you.

If you really want to give a man something right now, give him a little work to do.

Any man who is not moving a meaningful muscle to assist you in any tangible way—big or small—while having his way with you (whatever that may be), or *expecting* to have his way with you, is intentionally withholding from you. It's not an accident. It's no oversight. He didn't forget. He's not oblivious. He just doesn't think you're worth it and hopes that you don't ask. It would be awkward for him if you did. And even more awkward for the both of you when he tells you *No*.

Let's stay there for a moment: with you asking . . . or not.

There comes a time in every budding, or dying, relationship where you have to be honest with yourself and ask the question . . .

Am I Afraid to Ask?

Are you? Truthfully, if you needed or wanted something that was important to you, would you be afraid to ask the guy that you're dating or sleeping with to help you out for fear that he'll think you're trying to use him, or play the *"'But I'm boinking you'* card"? If so, then that is a clear sign that you should not be sleeping with him now, or even *thinking* about sleeping with him in the future.

But I Don't Want Him To Think I'm Using Him, Or To Feel Obligated To Help Me Just Because We're Having Sex

Okay. First of all, let's do away with the "just" in that statement. Let's omit that word altogether, because the inclusion of it minimizes the very tremendous act of sleeping with him. (Yes. Having sex with somebody is still a tremendous act.) This unentitled mentality is akin to: *"Well, I don't expect him to let me borrow his car this one time just because I'm the one who bought it for him."* Uh . . . Yes, you do. Yes, you *should.* Yes. Yes. Yes!

Listen, there are certain expectations, both spoken and unspoken, that accompany the sex package. The "*Boinking Him* Bundle", if you will. And if you're still not convinced, think about it this way, would you be afraid to ask a man that you're *not* sleeping with to assist you (e.g. a coworker, an elderly neighbor, an acquaintance, a platonic friend)? Would you think twice about asking one of these people to help you move, or to check under your hood because you heard something strange on your way to work? Most likely you wouldn't be the least bit reluctant. But throw in some sex and suddenly you cower at the mere thought of making him put to work a little perceived "pay for play". We cringe at our audacity to fix our mouths to ask even the smallest favor of the one we're letting rub all over us. Because the worst thing for us may be that he does, indeed, show his true colors and *actual* feelings for us and says what we feared: *No.*

When a man we've warmed up to tells us *No* when we ask a favor of him it hurts our feelings, but mostly, it embarrasses us. We're embarrassed to know the truth about him and how he feels about us. We're devastated to learn that he is not interested in us and our well-being the way that we hoped he'd be, and that he is, very likely, only interested in our vagina.

Worse than the *No-sayer*, a certain type of man may even resent you asking in the first place because now he's gotta reveal to you his *sleazebaggyness*. His thoughts sound something like this: *Damn her! She's making me show my true nature! Now she knows who and how I really am. Guess I won't be getting into those panties (anymore). Oh, well. Do I still have Jenna's number in my phone?*

Yep. Let him call Jenna. Because you should have no interest in a man like him. One who cares so little about you, who wouldn't flex a finger to help you. And might I add, you shouldn't have to ask in the first place. Not when the need is obvious to him.

That's all. We're done with that.

Which brings me to this:

Be clear on what you are looking to accomplish when getting involved with a man. If you are looking for sex and nothing more from a particular man, be upfront. The both of you should be upfront. Tell him. (In your own special way, of course. Not *"Hey, you! Wanna smash?"*) But, anything short of you *telling* a man this it goes *without* saying that you want more. He *knows* that you are looking to see if he is the special someone with whom you can eventually enter into a meaningful relationship. Again, unless you've stated otherwise, he knows good and well you're looking for something serious.

Men know that women want to be involved in a close, intimate relationship with one of them. They *know* this. Do not let a man try to play you later on with the, "*Oh, I'm sorry. I had no idea. I thought we were just having fun. You know . . . Hanging out'* phrase" accompanied by a look that's intentionally designed to make you feel like an over-presumptuous, desperate idiot. In other words, he's trying to, now, say (always *after* sex has taken place, I should note) that he had absolutely no idea in the world that you would want to actually *date* him seriously.

No man has ever told a virgin—or a VTH (That's 'Virgin To *Him*', meaning while she may not be an *actual* virgin, *he* hasn't had sex with her yet.)— "*Oh, I thought we were just taking things slow*" or "*I think that we should really take things slow, Shellanie.*" All of this "confusion" and brake-pumping comes only *after* he has explored her "inner world" with his "outer probe". Never before. *Never.*

Let's get back to Bob, or aka Mr. Inconsiderate. Sometimes a man's inconsideration can take on a form almost as ugly as the look you should give him when it occurs to you that he wants to be worthless in your life. Take this, for example:

Lizette just received a text from Isaiah. It reads as follows:

```
Isaiah: Hey
```

Lizette: Hey

Isaiah: I saw you the other day

Lizette: When?

Isaiah: The day after i left your place. You know the day you did that cool move on me with the ice cubes? The day after that.

Lizette: Oh yeah. Last Thursday

Isaiah: Yeah

Lizette: Where did you see me?

Isaiah: At the bus stop. I was driving down Blue Fin Rd on my way to the movies. You know, treat myself to a matinee. You know how we both love Transformers. Go Optimus! lol

Lizette: Yeah. I do love transformers. Long live Bumble Bee!! lol so, um, you saw me sitting at the bus stop?

Isaiah: Yep

Lizette: Oh

Mmm . . . hmm. Yep. The man rode right past her in his air-conditioned vehicle the day her car wouldn't start and she'd discovered her emergency roadside service membership had expired. Not that she'd called him back to her place to assist or anything. She knew that was a no-no. After all, she wouldn't want to put him out or inconvenience him, or worse, make him think she actually expected for him to treat her like a person he cares about. So, she broke in her new thong sandals and walked a half mile to the bus stop. As the tender webbing between her big toe and its closest neighbor throbbed in pain, he saw her sitting there, on the bench, sweating on that 97-degree-high-humidity-index day. She was sweating almost as much as he was on top of her just the day before that, pounding away. Yes, he saw her sitting there in need, and he didn't have the decency to offer her a lift.

Meanwhile, Mr. *Go Optimus!* is very likely still being expelled from her system. (I don't mean to be overly-graphic, ladies, but you *know* what I'm talking about. "Leftovers" from a low-quality man could, literally, still be trickling from a woman's body, and the lowlife in him won't even offer her a free ride on a heat-stroke-threatening summer's day. Should that be the man who gets her goodies? No, I say!

Which brings me to . . .

A man Before Sex, or BS
(Acronym *and* pun both completely accidental, but very much appropriate.)

vs.

A man After Sex, or AS
(Anyone besides me feeling like I'm an *s* short on that one?)

BS - May I give you a ride, my darling? I know your car is in mint condition but, honestly, I don't mind driving you twelve hours out of state to go to your grandma's fourth wedding to her *first* husband. Let me just get a brand-new transmission built. (No worries. I was due anyway.) What time should I pick you up next Tuesday?

AS - Why can't you just walk to the hospital? It's just eighteen blocks away. My car shakes whenever I go over 60 mph, so I can't take the highway. It wouldn't be a comfortable ride for you. Let me know what the cardiologist says. Text me.

This scenario, of course, would involve a man who has no love for you, not even a little bit. He's just out to get from you whatever you're willing to give, and then get on with his life.

Okay, so let's talk about the *You* Before and After Sex.

You Before Sex: I'm not sure. Let me check my schedule. I think I'm teaching a workshop that day. I'll let you know if I'm free. If you don't hear from me, though, just go ahead without me. We'll catch up another time. I'm about to run into a meeting. Gotta go.

vs.

You After Sex: Yes, I'm available right this very moment. I'll have one of the nurses sew up this patient. Oh, you just want to come over to my place? OK. I'll whip up a five-course meal, change into my lingerie, and wait for you on the porch with a glass of your favorite cognac. I can't *wait* to see you. Drive safely—*Nurse!*

Smokescreen Mode

Often after sex—specifically, *premature* sex—a woman might feel insecure, worried, paranoid, guilt-ridden, semi-ashamed, panicked, yearning, and overly-preoccupied with thoughts of "him" and when he'll call again. Then, wanting to salvage herself, redeem herself, she goes into "Smokescreen mode". In her head it sounds like, *Oh, my gosh! I had sex with him. He thinks I'm easy now. Surely, he's not as infatuated with me as he was pre-sex. What have I done? OMG! I did* that?! *What can I do to make him want me the way he wanted me* before *the sex? What can I do to get back on his hot-for-me list?* Then, having these thoughts, she'll begin trying too hard, overdoing it, making a fool of herself all in the name of trying to help him forget that she had sex with him so soon.

Listen, we as women can't smokescreen that. So why try? He didn't forget. He *won't* forget. So don't worry about it. The more worried about it a woman grows the clingier she'll get, and the more allergic to her he'll become. He'll know what she's trying to do. He'll know she's trying to compensate for having done the dirty deed with him prematurely. That she's trying to, now, desperately reveal more aspects about herself— force herself upon him—in order to make up for giving so much of herself to him so soon. She won't fool him into starting fresh with her, or into making an early commitment to her. It just doesn't work that way.

If this woman is you, just be confident. Be your wonderful self. Don't get all paranoid. Don't grow regretful. If you start acting all weird about what the two of you have done, then he will sense it and begin to back off. Besides, a decent, mature guy won't have negative thoughts about you at all (as if he wasn't in the room too). Retain your fabulous self-image, keep it moving, and everything will be fine.

#7

Stop Saying *"I Love You"* First

The Smart Sound of Silence

I'll keep this relatively short.

No guy, after having been told *"I love you"* by a woman whom he's never told the same, has ever said or thought to say in response, *"You know, I'm so glad you said that because it just reminded me that I love you too!"*, followed by a passionate embrace and equally passionate kiss.

Uh . . . it's creepy. And I promise you'll feel like a jackass afterwards, especially since he won't say it back. Yes, that's right. He's not about to follow your lead. He knows that *he* should be the one to say it first, to *feel* it first, and to let it be known, if applicable. If he, indeed, loves you, but hadn't yet told you, you just stole his thunder. On the flip side, if such a pledge is made too soon, if you just couldn't help yourself after thirty hot calendar days of kissing on him, he'll know it's much too heavy of a declaration to be made so hastily. You're not helping him to come around to loving you in return. You're not speeding up his heart-softening process. By the contrary, you've just pulled his emotional emergency brake. He's burning rubber until he's finally riding on the rims! And those aren't the kind of sparks you want flying.

On top of not needing a reminder or nudge, a man just simply doesn't need you telling him something so awkward. Like inappropriate complimenting, it makes his sausage shrink. You may as well say it in the burliest, bass-containing voice possible, because that's how it sounds by the time it gets to his unexpectant ears. You'll sound like "Bubba in the Top Bunk" saying it, minus the sideburns and gold tooth.

Upon hearing your emotional pledge, that man in your life instantly breaks out into a cold sweat. Imagine, just moments before, his heart pounding with joy, as his arm is draped around you. The two of you are having a great time. Maybe you're at the Ray's game at Tropicana Field. Maybe you're checking out your favorite comedian at *The Improv*. Or maybe you're just staring up at the mirror on the ceiling in his one-bedroom condo, naked from the waist down. Wherever you are, no matter the setting, you telling a guy who has never told you that you love him will bring all joy, all relaxation, all comfort to a screeching halt. It is the *prelationship* kiss of death. Now he thinks you're weak. You're silly. You're weird. He thinks you're not as high quality as he'd originally believed. He could be wrong about it all, of course. But it's what he'll think. He'll believe that you don't have as much self-esteem, integrity, or even just the good sense God gave a gecko as he'd initially given you credit for.

The next phase of his trauma, coming milliseconds after his mental demotion of your *dateability* rating, is that he'll instantly become claustrophobic in your presence. The moment the surprise words *"I Love You"* freefall from your mouth, 150 square feet of living space falls off the room you're sharing with him. (Three hundred if you followed it up with a kiss on the cheek. Seven hundred if you looked into his eyes when you said it.) That luxury-sized living room of his just turned into the most microscopic studio apartment he's ever had the misfortune of occupying. And that nice, comfy king-sized bed the two of you are sharing suddenly feels like his childhood twin bed at his mommy and daddy's house. (The one with the Nerf basketball hoop over the headboard.) And *you,* my dear, suddenly feel like his old Saint Bernard, Brutus, taking up 80% of the mattress space, breathing big-dog breath into his nostrils. He longs for some fresh air. For you to give him some elbowroom, preferably from your *own* apartment, several miles away.

This illustration of confinement doesn't even begin to describe the feeling that overcomes a man when you give in to the moment and carelessly (because it *is* careless) blurt out something so inappropriate and ill-timed. Its creepiness factor is right up there with me crying after sex. I can blame it on the margaritas all I want, but I can never take it back. And he can never "unwitness" it.

My point: We've all had our crappy, sappy moments. Just don't do it again. Zip those lips. The only time you should ever tell a man who is not related to you that you love him is when those words are immediately <u>preceded</u> by "*Awww . . .* ", and more immediately <u>followed</u> by "*too*". Let's practice.

Awww . . . I love you too.

Perfect.

Part 4

Putting Your Bra Back On

Getting Things Back Under Control One Shoulder at a Time

Who says soft can't be strong?

Oh, *Snap* Yeah!

So now that you're clear on how to take off those hideous pants of yours, let's talk about putting your bra back on. Think about all the wonderful things your bra does for you. It keeps things together. Corrects your posture. It helps you look even better in your dresses and gives your curves more longevity. Bras are good. Very good. They're a marvel invention. I'm wearing mine right now. It's had my back for several years now. And even when the day comes when putting it on proves to be a saggy, draggy exercise in futility I'm still going to rock it. Because putting your bra on is more than a dressing routine, it's also a mindset.

Putting your bra on is a shift in a woman's thinking from apologetic and unsure of herself, to self-accepting and uncompromising when it comes to the men she lets into her life. She honorably accepts her position as the coveted and does not compromise or waver on her most uplifting beliefs about herself and her respective role in the romantic dance. She owns her power and femininity. Most of all, she embraces her intelligence *and* good old-fashioned common sense. She doesn't pretend that she's someone she isn't. And she goes full force expressing who she *really* is.

A part of putting your bra back on is in maintaining your composure. Keeping yourself together. It means controlling yourself. Not being easily "shook" when the ride gets a little rough. It means arming yourself with confidence and inner strength. Look at it as putting on your awesome armor. This next section offers additional strategies for you to implement in your journey from a former pants-wearing woman to a bra-snapping beauty.

Come along. All cup-sizes welcome.

A Cup Abstinence

Shop Full. Date Empty.

You know those Snicker's candy bar commercials that say "You're not yourself when you're hungry"? That's totally true. Likewise, maybe you're not yourself when you're lonely (aka *horny*). This is why it is so important that you don't go on a date with repressed sexual energy.

You probably know by now that going to the grocery store on an empty stomach is a terribly expensive, cart-full-of-empty-calories idea. So unless you enjoy racking up a triple-digit tab for stuff you normally wouldn't crave on your worst day you try to make sure your stomach gets the attention it deserves before the essential errand. Just as "hungry-shopping" is ill-advised the same goes for going on a date with pent-up passion flowing through your bloodstream.

The reality is that some of us can go a very long time, months—*years*, even—without sexual activity. I, myself, have frequently fasted in this fashion during several chapters throughout my life. Usually there are no truly harmful side effects from this other than the normal irritability, moodiness, and overall bitchiness that can occur. (Oh. Did I type that?) However, there is one, more serious side effect that can occur when you put that much time between you and a penis:

givingituptothewrongmanitis

You've waited. And waited. And waited. And then . . . *Bam!* You give it up to the wrong man for the wrong reason at the wrong time. Or maybe you'll be lucky. Maybe you'll give it up to the *right* man at the wrong time for the wrong reason. (I won't share those odds with you.)

Why take such a gamble?

My point: You gotta get that ghost up out of you *before* you go on a date. You have to release—purge—those pent-up urges before you get in the company of a man, quality or reject. There is only one way to do this. Yes . . . you must masturbate before the date.

Understandably, you may blush at this, or laugh. But I'm serious. If you, like me, have a habit of placing several years between you and a man's "manhood" then, before you step out that door, you'd better get to buzzing!

Masturbate before the date!

I'm so serious about this one that I'm tempted to get T-shirts printed, or hashtag it. You see, it is, unfortunately, too easy to succumb to urges in ways you didn't intend to. The body blocks the brain. Go on and blame it on biology. But if you want your future relationship with a particular man to have the chance to evolve in a healthy and happy way, save yourself the post-sex regret and conduct this pre-date activity. Afterwards, put on your baggiest undies and retain your modesty after your meal.

Understand that it is intentional that I placed this specific bra-hooking strategy *first,* as its power should not be underestimated. This is because after you have slept with a man, implementing any of the other strategies that follow will be especially challenging.

We all know it because we've lived it: sex changes everything. Once we have given ourselves to man, particularly prematurely, we have already lost the game, or any bargaining chips we may have had prior to doing so. This can be dangerous. Here's why . . .

It becomes all too easy to excuse bad behavior and accept even the planet's worst male

creature's shortcomings once you have already given up your girly goodies to him.

Things that you normally wouldn't even *think* about accepting, or dare overlooking, are now accepted, rationalized, and plain *denied.* We begin to betray ourselves. Accept far less than we deserve. A man can get away with some serious barbaric behavior once he's conquered us sexually. We will tolerate all sorts of inconsideration, treachery, and even downright abuse (on some level) once we find ourselves feeling the need to cling to "He With Whom We've Made Monkey Music".

I wish it weren't true, but there *is* something about us women (at least, a substantial portion of us) that makes us lose our good sense post coital. You see, pre-sex we're much more objective, scrutinizing, even filled with a healthy sense of conceit, superiority, and control. We feel we can afford to be more assertive, more discriminating, more demanding when it comes to how someone treats us, especially when we know how badly they want us. However, once that headboard gets to banging, *Oh Boy!* there goes our good wits. There goes our easy ability to dismiss a loser without a second thought. At that point, a guy could, literally, begin wearing a shirt that reads "I'm Such A Loser, and I Won't Treat You Right", and some of us would still be inclined to continue moving forward with him. Why? Because we had

> *Sex is like mental and emotional Krazy Glue. We tend to get all sticky and look to adhere ourselves to a man afterwards. The danger is that you can get glued to an awful guy just as easily as you could a good one once you've "gone there".*

sex with him, that's why. We had sex with him and now we don't want to feel like this new mark on our "sex transcript" has been recorded in vain. We're thinking, on some level of consciousness:

> *"Well, I've already given up my goodies to him. I can't just walk away from him now. Then it would've all been for nothing. I better stick around—no matter what."*

A sad soliloquy if I've ever read one.

Sad as it may be, we start handcuffing ourselves emotionally and mentally to this man we've slept with before we should have. We begin digging in our heels on some of the most insane relationships all in the name of justifying a lust-driven mistake; something we could've just chalked up to *"My bad"*, and put it, and him, behind us. Instead, we begin to pursue a relationship with someone who we, upon discovery of who he *really* is, wouldn't normally desire to be with. And we only do it because we feel as if it's too late to back out of it without losing something. So, we stay with a loser for longer than we should.

Do yourself a favor and keep those panties of yours on until you have a better idea of just who you're granting access into not only your sexual world, but, more importantly, your mental and emotional world. A horrible man can conjure up for you a psychological nightmare once you've given your goodies to him. Don't empower him that way.

Let Him Respect You, Not Reject You

This refraining from sex mission is not just for you. It really does the both of you a huge favor when you wait. As much as a man wants to have sex with you, what he wants even more is to be in the company of someone he can genuinely respect, admire, *and* anticipate. The sex will only fill his "give it up to me" glass. It won't fill his emotional glass. And, most importantly, whether or not he acknowledges this on a conscious level, he'll feel a little ashamed about it. He'll know that he might've messed up something potentially great. That he just "effed up" a potential fairytale. Surely, he wouldn't mention his little bed session with you to his mom the next day, now would he? Right. He's ashamed. Disappointed. He may feel somewhere in his soul that he's been a dirty little birdie, and he'll have a hard time unlinking you to that feeling. Depending on the guy, this may even morph into resentment, again, if only at a subconscious level. So now he's gotta distance himself from you. From the shame he's feeling. He ends up rejecting you. Do yourself a favor. Keep your clothes on.

B Cup Barometer

Request His Best, Then Assess

It may be his best, but is it good enough . . . for you?

Warning: As I stated earlier, this particular piece of advice is going to be a challenge to follow if you've already played The *Primate Booty Classics* with the man on your mind. (See *A Cup Abstinence.*) That's the bad news. But the good news is that with reasonable effort, support from good friends, and renewed willpower, you can certainly do it.

We shall begin our learning using a non-example.

Introducing Bare Minimum Barry

Bare Minimum Barry. Just a step up from his step-brother, Bob, he's the guy who spends a shamelessly-nauseating amount of time thinking of ways to shortchange and shortcut a date with you rather than going all out. He's a human calculator, calculating every minuscule investment he makes, or *won't* make, to woo you. He'll conduct little experiments, tests of sorts, to see just what he can get away with. He observes your reactions, right down to your blinks per second, in order to determine if he can skate by with next to nothing.

For example, though Barry might pass by a lovely little floral shop on his way to meet you for a date—it could even be on the right side of the street, no need to make a left turn or U-turn—he won't stop. The thought of flowers may actually cross his mind as he knows that buying them is customary as far as date etiquette. Yes, something inside him, that shred of residual decency that lies dormant, deep in his duodenum, elbow-nudges him and says, *Yes, man! Flowers* are *a good idea. Get her flowers, Barry. Go, Barry! Go, Barry! Go, Barry!* The inner voice cheers, doing the cabbage patch dance. But Barry here tells his gut to *shut!* That meddling little cheerleader isn't enough to make this guy pull over for peonies. His foot applies additional pressure to the gas pedal as he accelerates through the yellow light.

He arrives at your apartment and rings the doorbell. He can't wait to see you. He wonders if you'll be wearing some cute little capris that complement your curves, and if those sexy little toes of yours are still painted in his favorite shade of purple. You looked hot the night he met you, and he knows that seeing you again will be a real treat.

But though Barry here has high hopes of your looking good he, on the other hand, is wearing a shirt that wouldn't be able to identify an iron in a police lineup, and shoes that missed a month's-worth of shining. He thought about sprucing himself up a little for you, but then thought, *What the hay. It's just date with (You).*

The two of you are off. Your stomach growls ever-so slightly on your way to lunch. You told him you like seafood. That it's the best. He agreed. He loves a good crab cake. With mouth-watering anticipation, you sink shotgun into your seat as he drives to your delicious destination. While you ride you look around his car. There are crumbs everywhere, including your seat. There's dust on the dashboard, and his spare pair of shoes are competing with yours for some floorboard. You kick his crusty kicks out of your way and look out the window to enjoy the drive, but it's difficult hard to take in the scenery because there is a huge splat of bird poop on your window. You close your eyes for the rest of the drive.

Once the two of you pull up to the dining spot you wonder whether Jimmy's Fast & Hot Flounder is blocking the fine marine restaurant where you assumed you'd be dining. But nope. You've arrived. And Old Barry Boy parks right next to the mud-covered pickup truck with the two-toned doors and announces, *"We're here!"*

"It's my treat," he tells you at the 'Order Here' counter as he mistakes your purse readjustment for a money-searching maneuver. You smile and look around for a clean table while Barry stares up at the menu on the wall in search of some specials. He decides that asking for a cup of water and only ordering one fountain beverage will allow the two of you free refills for half the cost. Besides, the dollar movie theater he's taking you to afterwards will surely fetch, at least, five bucks or more for even the smallest soda. Barry won't dare dish out dollars like that. Drink up, girl.

You made it through lunch, and you survived the movie. When Barry drops you off back at home he thinks he's earned himself a little "kiss-kiss" for the night. After all, he broke down and let you get nachos at the theater, which he shared, of course. So, on your porch, he positions himself for a pucker. You look at him like he's crazy, and tell him you'd better get inside, that your boyfriend is probably back home by now. (Genius, by the way.) You hi-five his puckered face—*hard*—and dash inside your apartment, shutting the door on this miserly man.

This is the only way to handle this corner-cutting poor excuse for a wooer. He's a cheapskate in every sense of the word. Yes, he picked you up, but showed up empty-handed. Yes, he did the driving, in a filthy vehicle that he should've had detailed beforehand. Yes, he paid for lunch and a movie, but at an awkward bargain. At Jimmy's, when the cashier asked if he wanted to add two-for-one turnovers, Barry quickly shook his head *No*, frowning at the teenager like he wanted to rip his head off for even suggesting such a cross-sell.

Pre-Date Homework Tip #1

Know whether you'll be staring down at your menu, or up at it.

What you saw was Barry's best. But it was nowhere near being good enough for you. I say it was his best because it was the best that he was <u>willing</u> to give you. Don't let Bare Minimum Barry call the shots. Don't let him set the bar so low that a world-champion limbo dancer couldn't get underneath it. This guy can get you so horribly used to receiving next to nothing that one day he can show up to your house, yank up a weed from your yard, and shove it at you, dirt falling onto the porch. At this point, when you open the door you'd be so delighted at his "thoughtfulness" that you'll gasp, surprised, looking all starry-eyed, before falling into his arms weeping, *"What did I do to deserve you?"*

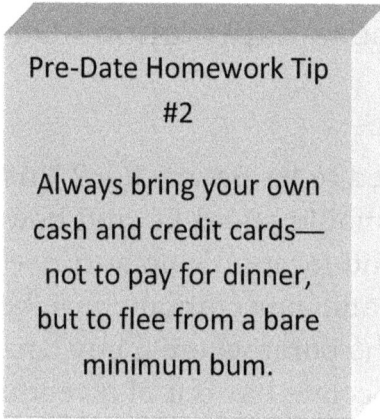

> Pre-Date Homework Tip
> #2
>
> Always bring your own cash and credit cards— not to pay for dinner, but to flee from a bare minimum bum.

Barry's A Big Boy

He Knows What He's Doing

Before you go feeling sorry for Barry, excusing his cheapskate ways, ask yourself: If this were his mother, sister, or future daughter would he tell either of them to accept the kind of low-budget treatment he expects you to accept from him? Record your answer below. (I've already gotten you started.)

Hell N _! *(Complete this response.)*

Get Those Expectations Off the Floor!

Still tempted to let Barry slide? Unsure about what you should stand for and how tall you should stand for it? It's no surprise. Your standards and expectations have been so under attack to the point where a guy could "karate kick" a chocolate bar out of a vending machine on Valentine's Day, and you'd consider him Cupid's Answer as you nibble on it, imagining yourself in a wedding gown and holding a bouquet that matches his cummerbund.

Where do we draw the line, ladies? Even hand-holding has got us crowning a guy "The One." When he holds our hand in public, we think the privilege is all ours. We are later on the phone with our friends, reliving the moment:

"He actually held my hand in public today!"

"Ooooh, he did??!!!!"

Yes!!!"

(Squeals)

Is that the new standard? I hope not. Otherwise, what's next?

"Girl, he actually let me have sex with him!"

"He did????"

"Yes!!!"

(Squeals)

Ladies, our expectations are on the floor, mashed into the grout! All steps to taking your pants off and putting your bra back on revolve around the central theme of raising your expectations back up to a respectable level, and this one's no exception.

We get what we expect to get. Expect a man to pamper you. Expect a man to treat you right. To respect you. And if he doesn't, expect to be perfectly okay after you drop him like an out-of-range call. A man giving you anything less than what you deserve, what you *require,* doesn't need to be in your energy field exchanging electromagnetic waves with you. A man has a choice of whether or not to pursue you, to stick around circling the outskirts of your life waiting to get in. If the plate that you lay out in front of you is too challenging for a particular man to step up to, then tell him to *Step Off!* No Bare Minimum Barries should ever gain entry into your lovely life.

An Ad Best Left Unanswered:

Attention:
Ladies

MAN "UP FOR GRABS"!

(Quality not
included.)

Asset or Asshole?

Sit back and let a man show you who he is. And then don't expect it to get any better.

Is the man on your mind an asset? *What's an asset,* you ask? Well, an asset, in terms of dating, is someone who adds value to your life. Someone who enhances your life in some significant way. For example, is he a great companion? Is he easy to be with? Are conversations with him stimulating, and do they promote your growth? Does he leave you feeling good, and like you're a better person after having spent time with him? Is he able to help you in practical ways? *Does* he help you in practical ways? Oh, *he does,* you say? Well the man on your mind just may be an asset.

So, What's an Asshole?

An asshole is someone who has little to no respect for you (and usually others). This person is self-centered, selfish, and, in some cases, downright evil. This is not a person who will try to uplift you or enhance your life experience in any way. Instead, this person is only interested in satisfying whatever basic, if not sadistic, urges they may have, and you, to them, are a potential source of such satisfaction. Such urges may include, for example:

- the urge to criticize

- the urge to demoralize

- the urge to downright torture

Though they come in various forms, let's look at two, more common, examples of an Asshole.

Meet Mr. *Not-Funny*

Does he criticize you in the name of "humor", and when you get offended, follow up with *"I was just kidding. Geesh! You can't take a joke? Loosen up!"*?

Well, what did he say exactly? Let's have a look.

"Sarah, you look ridiculous in that skirt. What year is that from? 199-Eww!?"

Just because *he* laughed after insulting you doesn't make it "a joke". It only makes him an asshole, who, by the way, would just be getting started on what's sure to end up becoming a constant stream of criticism of you. Tons more insults. Loads more "laughs". He's merely giving you a preview of what's to come. He's just warming up on putting you down.

Other Indicators:

Do his punchlines make you want to punch *him*?

Are *all* of his "jokes" about you? In other words, has he ever made a joke about anything else *besides* you, or are you always the subject of these comic fails? And by the way, are these "jokes" about you even funny? Probably not. They are only funny to him because he enjoys insulting you, chipping away at your self-esteem so that you feel less good about yourself than you did before you met him. Then you begin to feel "lucky" to have *him* in your life—you know, with you being so hideous and all. Get this joker off the stage.

I mean, we can all laugh at ourselves. It's fun to let our hair down and not take ourselves so seriously sometimes. But it's best to heckle this Jekyll right out of your life.

Meet Mr. *Oh, Did You Want Something Too?*

We dropped in on him earlier, sipping his Café con Selfish. This one doesn't consider you at all. And if he does, if the thought does happen to cross his mind to take care of you in some small way, he quickly dismisses it. You are not his priority in any sense of the word. Kick him to the curb. Garbage Day is tomorrow. Don't recycle this one. To the landfill he goes!

Jokes aside, you seriously must consider after having spent a significant amount of time with a man what his contribution to your life will be and whether it's sufficient or not. Even in the early stages, there are some clear-as-day signs of what's to come. Is it what you've envisioned for yourself? The partnership you've dreamed of? If not, do yourself a favor and stay single until you find what you know you need *and* deserve.

Loyal To A Lowlife

There's another type of asshole worth mentioning. A more malignant type. His evil runs through and through. He *bleeds* disharmony. And while you may not be the specific target of his torture, he's an asshole to society no less. He is the lowlife. His many manifestations of evil are all void of mercy, tolerance, and Good as we know it. But, sadly, even this type of asshole can snag a woman to slink by his side. She sees his dirt. She knows his tremendous harm done. But she narrows her focus to only consider who he is for *her*. The world can go to hell.

Don't be this woman. Lose the Lowlife and get on with yours.

Bad "Row"mance

Disgustingly, even serial killers have admirers and receive love letters and fan mail from women who look past, or even lust over, their heinous crimes and terrorism against society. Some of these sociopaths may even get married while sitting on Death Row. Now that's just *bride-diculous!*

You don't want to be considered the closest thing to one of these brain-challenged brides. Being loyal to a lowlife, I might add, puts you on a trajectory of eventually marring the Hubby from Hell—for better or for *hearse.* Don't be *bridesperate!* Leave these top-level losers alone.

Single and *Desperate* are not synonyms

World's Worst Pre-Proposal

A very handsome, very educated, very successful man once offered to "fast track" me. This was his way to describe speeding up the *getting to know me* phase and, ultimately, making me his wife in record time. *"I'm trying to fast track your ass!"* was what he *actually* said to me during a heated disagreement. Besides the inherent craziness of this statement, he was also a pretty rude person in general. My response: *Uh... No Thanks.*

He's Not Living Up To Your Dreams And Expectations? Then,

Go Ahead. Change That Man!

Take Those Pants Off And Put Your Bra Back On!

Contrary to what you may have heard, you *can* actually change a man. Read on to find out more.

Take Those Pants Off And Put Your Bra Back On!

Yes, you read that right. You can transform that man of yours—*Instantly!* Here's how . . .

Take Those Pants Off And Put Your Bra Back On!

While, admittedly, there is only one way to change a man, this one way is tremendously effective. Ready to learn how? Here it is . . .

Take Those Pants Off And Put Your Bra Back On!

You can transform him from USELESS to

YOU-LESS.

Ta-dah! He's a changed man. You did it!

Now wasn't that easy?

Take Those Pants Off And Put Your Bra Back On!

Argument for Transforming That Man

Why waste your time trying to figure out how to change a man who is treating you in ways far less than what you deserve? Why live life frustrated over a guy who can't, or just *won't*, make any attempt to meet your most basic and essential needs in a relationship be it security, honesty, emotional intimacy, loyalty, etc.? Just as you can't control him, you also cannot change him. You can't change his character, his tendencies, or his treatment of you. You can't force him to "act right", "be decent", "be helpful", "be considerate", "stay faithful", or anything else that may be important to you.

Therefore, it stands to reason that if you are seeking a change to take place as it relates to that man of yours, then changing him from *Useless* to *You-less* is truly the only way to go. Transform him from being *in* your life, to being *out* of your life.

Change is good.

A manner-less man should be a womanless man. Likewise, a useless man should be without your attention, company, and time.

Poof-be-Gone *him.* **ASAP!**

C-Cup Common Sense

Date *Him*, Not Yourself

I've got some breaking news for you:

Paying attention to your date can really pay off.

Getting to know someone requires you paying attention to *that* person, not paying attention to how you're coming across, or looking, to that person. In our overly-self-conscious worlds we may find ourselves focusing more on ourselves when on a date instead of the man sitting across from us. We must remember that a date is an opportunity for us to learn something about the other person. Self-consciousness is a barrier to that effort. When we focus on ourselves we can miss out on some crucial facts—critical clues about the other person's character.

Here are some things you may be focused on instead of him:

-Talking more about yourself

Um ... you already know *you*. You know *you* better than anyone else in the world. Use this time to get to know *him*.

-**What you look like**

Was there a mirror in your house or apartment? Is there one in your purse? Check it and be done, because I'm sure you look fine. Now, how does *he* look?

-**What he's thinking about your looks**

If you think you look great then so will he. Confidence is funny that way.

-**How you look eating**

Just chew. Dab. Repeat. Your mastication skills are to be envied.

-*What* **you're eating**

Hey. You ordered it. Dig in!

-**What he thinks about how you look eating.**

See Mastication 101 above.

-**How you sound talking**

Like music to his ears.

-**What you should say next**

Whatever socially-appropriate thing that comes to mind.

-Whether he's interested in you enough to ask you out again

Baby steps here. Get back to *this* date.

It's hard to assess a man when you're too busy assessing yourself. Try to avoid this self-criticizing practice during dates with a prospective mate. Instead try to make a conscious effort to focus on who and how *he* is. What he reveals about himself in words and actions. What kind of person is he? You already know who and how *you* are. What about him? What have you learned about him so far? What have you discovered that moves him either up the interest scale or slides him down a notch? Wouldn't it suck to get home with a belly full of food and realize you don't know the guy you just shared the evening with any better two hours and 1200 calories later than you did before the two of you sat down? It would really stink to find out that you learned almost nothing about him because you were on a date with your own thoughts about yourself.

Enjoy him. Enjoy yourself. Enjoy the moment.

Scrutinize him, not yourself!

Take Those Pants Off And Put Your Bra Back On!

D-Cup Dignity

The (Missing) Eleventh Commandment:

Thou shalt not claim thee who doth not claim thou.

If you can't handle the truth you might want to skip this part. Better yet, don't skip it. Read it. *Twice.* This is where I take the gloves off and be "BFF honest" with you.

We saw in the last section the importance of using precious dating time to scrutinize the man with whom you're out. It is of even greater importance, however, that a woman keep her eyes, ears, and heart fixed on the *right things,* the heavy hitters, lest she get distracted by the minor, less important details and characteristics of a man such as his looks, sense of humor, or precise height and weight. Yes, those things can be icing on the cake. But they're not *the cake.*

In the same vein, we shouldn't be so easily turned off by superficialities on a material level. We must avoid tallying up in our minds the cost of his watch, or sunglasses, or shoes. Forget his wack watch. To hell with his discount shoes. The first and foremost turn-off for you should be a man who doesn't want *you.*

Yes. Yes, ladies. This may sound like a no-brainer, but, believe me, it isn't. The man who doesn't give a damn about you is too often the one who leaves you yearning for more of his ambivalence and torture. For some reason, you want him to give a damn about you. You want his attention. Your ego, your fragile sense of security, needs this *nobody* to say or act in a way that validates you, that says "You're special". But instead he couldn't care less about you.

Sometimes this cold demeanor is deliberate. Several men have read some variation of the *'How to Be an Asshole'* books. While titles, of course, don't contain this particular term, they all endeavor to teach men specific strategies for mastering the art of intentionally mistreating women in order to make us curious enough, or insecure enough, to desire them (more). This is probably some of the only reading many of these men have done since middle school but, more committed to the mission of torturing you than genuine literacy and education, they have earmarked those particular pages that encourage them to mishandle women as a means to attract and lure them in greater quantities with greater frequency.

Admit it. How many of us have been guilty of pursuing a man who never wanted us, or didn't want us anymore? We don't have to raise our hands. But we do have to raise our standards and self-esteem.

Don't wince. Don't get sensitive over my tone here. I'd rather embarrass you now, in the solitude and safety of your own home and mind, than have you embarrass yourself publicly, in front of "him", and others. Never chase down some guy who is clueless to your worth and awesomeness.

Now the fact that I say you are worthy and awesome does not mean that you should now make it your mission to show "him" just *how* worthy and awesome you are. If he doesn't already know or suspect this then he is a dummy in your world. It is not your job, or duty, or responsibility, or appointed act of sainthood to bring him to the realization of your wonder and greatness by calling him and telling him all about it, or by flaunting another man in his face. Just leave him alone, and busy yourself with something (or someone) better.

Bottom line: Don't fall for it. Don't be fueled by a guy's aloofness. His ambivalence stinks. His bad boy persona is sour. If he's not chasing you then back away from him.

Pseudo Beau Delusional?

We all love a good romance. Heart-warming motivation to rise in the morning. What better inspiration to make you see the good in the world than being with a romantic partner? Partnerships can really make our worlds go round. They feel, well, better than anything.

But are you being delusional about your "partnership"? Are you sure it's solid and substantial? Are you sure this man on your mind is really "with you"? Is he into you the same way that you're into him? Or are you pretending to believe he is? Creating your own little fantasy?

It's so easy to pretend that we're loved when things are light and going "OK". (Notice I didn't say "well"). We can easily rate a romance a 10 out of 10 when there is nothing to lose, or nothing real and heavy. It feels good to *feel* loved, even if you know that if you paused for a moment and reflected on the relationship for even two seconds you'd have to admit that it isn't anywhere near as real as you tell people it is, or as you try to tell yourself.

The mere thought of the true state of your relationship may make you shudder. Perhaps it gives you a heart-dipping sting that makes you, surprisingly, clutch tighter to the arm of your "pseudo beau" because it still feels good to pretend so long as you don't consciously admit it to yourself. But you *are* pretending. And you know it.

You know damn well that's not your man!

You may call it "going with the flow". And it is. You are flowing down a river of fantasy because, *my gosh!* it feels so good. But in the end, when it's over, and you do take some time to think, you sink, because on top of hurt, humiliated, and rejected, you are also ashamed of yourself for letting things get this way because you knew all along that you were pretending and that none of it was ever real. (Are we still BFFs? I hope so, because that was said out of love.)

I'm not saying not to have your fun. Go ahead. Have your fun. I'm just saying be honest with yourself and stay fully aware of what things really are. What a situation really is. Maybe it's your fun little fantasy. Lavish in it. But don't forget the truth. Don't set yourself up for an unnecessary fall. Know what you're involved in and proceed as you wish in a fully aware state of mind.

Speaking of being truthful with yourself . . .

Chump from Jump

As just discussed, there are times when we lie to ourselves outright. But other times, it's more . . . um . . . *evolutionary.* I mean, we know what the real deal is at first, but later we second-guess ourselves, before ultimately arriving back at our initial impressions.

The Wrong Sandwich:

When We *Knew* Better!

Have you ever made the wrong sandwich? I don't mean making a Ham & Swiss when you should've made a PB & J. I'm talking about getting with a guy you knew full well from the very start was bad news. Let me explain.

Once upon a time there lived Ms. Beautiful Woman, who thought very highly of herself. She knew her worth, and took pride in her femininity, whole-heartedly embracing her role as the coveted. Then along came Peter Little. He'd read all the psychology books. He was a champion poker player. He was a man who had nothing to lose. But, above anything else, he was lazy. He wanted Beautiful to accept next to nothing when it came to him. Beautiful refused this nonsense. This ridiculousness. Peter spoke with his actions (or inaction) and Beautiful, naturally, refused to accept this.

In the beginning.

From the very start Beautiful knew something was not right about Mr. Little in terms of what he was proposing through his actions or lack thereof. Like a poisonous plant that looks very well poisonous she noticed the obvious toxicity of this particular man. The skull and crossbones label practically appeared on his forehead above the very word: POISON. So, as any sane woman would, she turned up her nose to him. Shunned him. And rightly so.

But then one day, after all this noticing and shunning, Beautiful, for some strange reason (perhaps loneliness, or boredom), decided to give this unpalatable person a try. She'd concluded that he *was* worth her time, believing she'd initially misread him. Overriding her intuition, deciding that her first impression of him couldn't be trusted, she cocked her head to the side, squinted her eyes, chewed on her bottom lip and said to herself "I think he's actually a great guy. I'm going to date him." She forfeited her good sense and took a ride with this low-quality guy. A ride that turned out to be quite turbulent.

Inevitably, much sooner than later, this guy of hers showed his true colors and proved himself to be every bit of rotten as her first impression of him said he was, or would be. She was right about him the first time. But now it's too late. She's been hurt. And the long journey of healing (a period of time that, unfortunately, is usually much longer than the actual length of the relationship) has only just begun.

While there are certainly exceptions, most men aren't that suave. Casanova he may be, but Don Juan he is not. Most of the time these low-quality men are practically wearing face tats that scream with caps lock enabled—in 100-point, bold, underscored font— **_"PLAYER"_**, or **_"USER"_**, or **_"CHEATER"_**. But it's the occasional sweet gesture, or seemingly-shared interests or philosophy of life that makes us ignore what we know or suspect him to be. It's the compliment that comes across as so sincere. So genuine and heart-felt, simply because it's what we wanted to hear but didn't expect. It's the unexpected instance of decency, of normalcy, that makes us imagine the wolf's fangs gradually shrinking down to become normal-sized, filed-down canines right before our very eyes. It's an optical illusion, ladies. Our loneliness is a lousy source upon which to rely when it comes to providing us with the soft data that is required to analyze a situation and decide upon an appropriate mate. His deception in this case would really be more a matter of our own projection.

This kind of self-deception can occur easier than we think. We see a guy and, immediately, though he may appear somewhat attractive, or intriguing, we see something else in him. Something sneaky, or just "off". We *see* it. In that quick moment we eliminate him as a potential *anything* in our lives. Our intuition, or just plain eyesight, called him out. Told on him. Told us he wasn't right.

The Recipe

So, we've seen this disqualifying quality (or qualities) in him right off the bat. That's our first slice of bread: seeing the truth. The truth being he's not good enough for us. That he's bad news.

But then something happens. We start letting him charm us with his conversation. Or maybe he turns out to be smart and, this, for some reason, surprises us, so he starts scoring points with us because of this. We think *"Oh, Wow. I didn't know he was so smart."* (As if assholes can't be smart.) And then we think, *"Hmmm.... maybe he's awesome* after all". We let other, often times, insignificant things about him distract us and lure us toward someone who we sensed from the very beginning—before he even opened his mouth—was not good for us.

It could be as simple as him smelling good or helping us out with a problem at work that's been driving us nuts. Whatever it is it's a distraction. A red herring. We saw something shiny in him, and now, suddenly, we're painting him "perfect for us". That second determination is the filling. The meat. The protein, if you will. This is what will be in the middle on top of that first slice of bread. It's the lie. The deception. The fraud.

Now we're dating him. And soon we're giving up our goodies to this guy. Meanwhile, we're thinking one thing, and he's thinking another.

But things don't feel good after a while. Usually sooner than later. But we keep talking ourselves into him, withstanding the pain and frustration he inevitably brings, until one day, one of us (usually him) decides to end the torture of being together. And this is when we finally realize that we were right about him all along. That he was nothing but trouble. That realization is our second slice of bread. That second layer of truth. And it matches the first slice. Our sandwich is complete.

We ladies often kick ourselves later, telling ourselves that we should've never trusted him. That we should've relied on our instincts to begin with. That we should have gone with our gut. This is never really a Eureka moment for us, though. It's a *"Gosh! Why Didn't I Trust My First Impression of Him?!"* Moment.

Eureka? No. More like, Eu-Knew-It all along.

I've made plenty of wrong sandwiches in my life. They taste awful. Swallowing your own *I-told-you-so's* is a sure way to get indigestion. But pop an antacid and let it fizz, because it's actually great for our emotional and psychological development to reflect on the ways in which we've trusted some loser instead of our own intuition and common sense. We come to realize that it wasn't him. It was us. We fooled ourselves. Then, eventually, we'll ask ourselves why. And that's when the real healing begins. Wrong sandwiches produce great wisdom.

Bra-Clamations

Here's a recap of what to tell yourself when you're ready to put your bra back on:

❖ I will keep my legs closed to those I don't know. And, in the event I should "slip up", I will not handcuff myself to a man just because he saw me naked.

❖ While my legs are closed, I will carefully scrutinize a man, and then make sound decisions based upon my thorough observation and evaluation of him.

❖ I will stand by my standards—free of guilt—and only invite into my life those quality relationships I know that I deserve.

❖ I will not waste my time (and life) entertaining an asshole.

❖ I will not throw myself upon a man, or mislabel him as "mine", especially when he doesn't claim or want me in return.

❖ I will know when a man is BSing me and, more importantly, when I am BSing myself.

T. L. BROWN

Take Those Pants Off And Put Your Bra Back On!

Part 5

Not So Fast

So, He's Won You Over, What Exactly Did He Win?

It takes two. And that includes you.

Take Those Pants Off And Put Your Bra Back On!

What's In It For Him?

He's won you over. The two of you like each other. Depending on the length and quality of the relationship, you may even *love* each other. You get one another. You appreciate each other. You both have decided that the other is a wonderful companion. That's great.

So, now that we've talked about what we, as women, should require from those sniffing around our lives, it's time to talk about what's in it for them. By "in it" I mean *the perks*. Presumably the relationship's foundation is solid enough (e.g. built upon mutual trust, respect, and a genuine appreciation of the other), but the *perks* are what takes a romantic experience with another person from good to spectacular! Everybody loves perks.

Now, while I am a firm (sometimes to a fault) believer that men should behave like gentleman by, in part, doing all the things I've mentioned in this book, I would be remiss if I didn't discuss more about you, the woman, and your lift in a new or established relationship.

Bestow Upon Your Beau

I knew a woman who was rather crabby and a touch too bossy. Actually, she was downright unpleasant to be around on a semi-regular basis. She wasn't the embarrassingly-typical "magazine cover beauty", and during conversations barely let anyone else get in a word edgewise. Loud and obnoxious, her personal appeal ranked amongst the lowest, from my limited, outside perspective. I wondered, then, for all of ten seconds, how it was that she had tons of friends, but, mainly, what she had to offer the man in her life who had put up with her for so long, as they had been married for decades and had adult children.

I soon realized, as I lingered in her company, that she was an excellent cook. On top of that, she seemed to whole-heartedly *enjoy* the act of feeding her family. Cooking and serving brought out her joyful, softer side. Her meals may not have been gourmet, but they were hot and frequent, and made her family very happy.

That reliable home-cooking that she provided for her family was, no doubt to me, one of the wonderful things about her that made her lovable. I imagined it helped to offset some, if not all, of that bossiness that may rub some the wrong way. I grew to believe that even *I* would take some crap from her if she fed me that way on a regular basis, as I still have dreams about that banana pudding.

I am sure she had other delightful qualities, but her cooking was the one her husband talked about most when he'd come around to mingle at our company's holiday celebrations. It was clear that her strong *"pots and pans"* game came with her *"Mrs. Bossy Pants"* package, and it made her more appealing than she would have been otherwise in my eyes. Surely her husband was with her for more substantial reasons (i.e. emotional), but I'm sure the cooking didn't hurt. Without her culinary skills and willingness to use them who knows exactly how socially bearable she would've been.

> # I AM <u>NOT</u> TELLING YOU TO GET YOUR BUTT IN THE KITCHEN.

Many a drive-thru have caught me on camera, sometimes twice a week, screaming into a speaker, so it's not about "cooking", specifically. While I clearly believe in the woman's role as "the coveted and chased" in a *pre*lationship, I am not, under any circumstances, going to identify for you your technical role in a relationship, or your *perk plays*. That would be wrong on so many levels. Some women enjoy cooking. Some don't. Some enjoy keeping an enviously-clean home with a twist of OCD organization. Some do just fine curling up with a book with a pile of dishes in the sink.

Some women are natural entertainers and hostesses. Others may be more reclusive and better adept at setting up scenes for more intimate time together. And the list goes on. All are fine. You know yourself and your proclivities. Now go ahead and let them shine. And if it's not too much trouble for you, bestow their benefits upon your beau. Treat him to whatever it is that *you* do from the heart.

Be Considerate & Thoughtful

Think about the long-term man in your life in ways that you hope and expect him to think about you. For example, if you see something cool while you're out and about that you just know he'll love, why not grab it? Make his day! A shopper like me finds this fun and exciting. I love picking up things for the man in my life that I know will surprise and delight him all at once. Let your natural generosity shine. Don't suppress it. You're generous and thoughtful for a reason. Those qualities shouldn't stop short at the man you're seriously involved with.

Note: I could throw up a caution sign here, warning you to be careful about whom you shower with such gifts. But if the certified man in your life has shown you his G-Spot already, then go for it! If he's your tried and true, solid and steady man then he deserves to be treated the same way that he treats you.

Knowing When and When Not

Step 1: Distinguish between a man you've just met and are still getting to know, and a man you've been enjoying life with for a good while.

Step 2: Differentiate your treatment accordingly.

So go ahead, do nice things for him. If you know he likes or appreciates certain things, and you don't mind catering to him these things, by all means *do*. If he likes fishing in shallow, muddy, murky waters, well, "wader up" and go with him. You bring the worm! If you know that he has a strong affection for confection, hit up his favorite sugar shop once in a while, then grab a fork and playfully feed him as if it were you on that lucky piece of silverware instead. If he wants his hair bleached and styled in a long, crazy plait in the back, show him that cosmetology class you took back in high school wasn't a total waste in your schedule. (Then show him your best "buzz cut work" afterward.) Make him smile. Make him feel good about life when he's with you. Everyone deserves to feel good and enjoy comfort in their lives. Relationships are supposed to enhance our lives, raise the quality. Provide that good man of yours with some comfort and convenience by virtue of being involved with you. Make it a terrific two-way street. What are you willing and able to do to help your man feel good today?

You have another power. You have the power to make another person feel good. That might even be a superpower.

But What If He Begins Taking Me for Granted?

That's an easy one. Just stop doing all those wonderful things that you do for him and see if he "notices".

Because, after all, he, too, should learn the words "Thank You" `—and mean them!

First Know Your Worth. Then Make It Work

In order to authentically, confidently, and comfortably bestow upon your beau you must know thy self. You must know what you bring, *first*, to your own life, and from there consider what you may naturally bring into the life of someone else. If you don't happen to know your talents, your strengths, the things that you are naturally great at, then it is important that you take a few moments to figure it out. (Begin brainstorming below. I'll wait . . .)

> ### Ways That I Rock!:
>
> 1.
> 2.
> 3.
> 4.
> 5.

Why not make yourself useful to the one you cherish?

Continue your brainstorming with making mental notes throughout the week of all the things you have to offer. Flip that imaginary piece of paper over and write on the backside too! Know your worth. And don't worry if your mental list doesn't seem like something that a specific man would enjoy or appreciate. Have faith and stand firm that only the type of man *who would* find your gifts to be the precious ones that they are is the type whom you'll, possibly, grant access into your world. Remember, this is not for you to go out and acquire new "skills" in order to make yourself more marketable or desirable to a particular man. I'm talking about taking inventory of all the wonderful attributes that you already possess that a man may, too, enjoy. This way you can be confident in knowing that you are, indeed, a catch. He's not doing you any favors by "letting you" date him. The two of you are serving *each other* in ways that both of you (can) appreciate.

Oh, Count the Ways . . .

Don't be shy about acknowledging your strengths, talents, and value. Every woman is magical in her own way. It may be your kindness and loving spirit that stands out more than the average person's. Maybe you're an active humanitarian, or a tremendous help to those around you. Perhaps you are a continuous source of motivation or inspiration to those in your circle. You may have a natural knack for uplifting the people around you through humor, or honest counsel. Be bold about what you bring. I imagine that you are valuable in a multitude of ways. The important thing is to know it. Know what it is that you stand to provide for someone else, what they stand to gain by virtue of being in your presence. Being in your life should be a treat for a man. Know how so.

While we learn more about ourselves with every year of life, and from every relationship we experience, a fundamental practice should be to take shameless inventory of our personal attributes. Knowing your special brand of value as someone in a relationship is essential, so don't rush this process. Really take the time to think about it. Take as long as you need to fully capture all that is great about you. When you know what you bring to another person, the ways in which you willingly nourish, enhance, and provide for the other, you'll never question your worth in a relationship. You'll never second-guess your degree of worthiness in someone else's eyes or run the risk of allowing someone to undervalue you.

Don't Mind Being Kind

When it comes to relationships, half the joy is in giving. Giving the best of ourselves can be truly rewarding for our partners *and* our own spirits.

People today pretty much agree that self-care is essential to all aspects of our health. It's impossible to really give when we are neglecting ourselves in significant ways. However, when we can understand that life isn't *just* about focusing on ourselves, fulfilling our own personal needs, or accomplishing our "brag-worthy" ambitions, but, instead, looking outside of ourselves sometimes, and pouring positive action and energy into others, that's when the fruit—the seed—that lies within us can grow an orchard of goodness.

When we choose to embrace the philosophy that we don't live exclusively for ourselves and begin to support and love others in ways that are beneficial to them, we can feel more accomplished, more significant, more powerful than we ever have. Find your superb, irresistible "thing" and pamper your man away. But remember, it has to be something that you truly *enjoy* doing. Something you don't mind doing. It can't feel like a chore. It must be something you can do with relative ease and, most importantly, something you're able to do long term. No bait and switch here, ladies. That wouldn't be fair. Now, would it?

Women Should Treat a Good Man Like He's a Good Man:
The Basics

While, again, I refuse to make generalizations that border on sexist or stereotypical as it applies to women and what we can provide should we choose to bestow upon our beau, I do, however, believe in some *universals*, if you will. Some basics.

Is he a gentleman? Is he treating you well? Thoughtful? Generous? Considerate? Then go ahead and reward him with some reciprocity. Respond to his tender loving care with some tender loving care!

Well, how do I do that??? you may ask.

I have a short answer and a long answer for that.

Treat the man in your life the way that you will want your future son's girlfriend or wife to someday treat him.

That was the short answer.

What follows over the next few pages is the long answer.

1. Be Mindful of Your Mood

Moody much? Relationships are not dumping grounds for the myriad of emotions that may move through you throughout the day. It's not fair for anyone to take out their frustrations on their partner. This goes for both women and men. This may be a habit—a bad one—so be mindful. Try to catch yourself when you're doing this. I, personally, have been involved with some moody men in my past. O-M-G!!! This was excruciating. Being around someone who puts you on edge can drive you crazy. It's neither fun, nor healthy. And it certainly wasn't my destiny, so I got the hell up out of there—*pronto!*

2. Give Him What He Wants and Needs

Security takes on many forms and means different things to different people. For some, it's financial security they crave. For others, it's a warm, loving, comfortable home. One that smells good, sounds good, looks good, and feels good to be in.

Not everything matters that much to everybody. What warms one person's heart may not raise the temperature of another's by a single degree. The man in your life may not care about the house being spick and span. He may like the "lived-in" look. So, what *does* he care about? What floats his boat? Find out. Study your man. Know his desires. What makes him *happier*? Tailor it to him. Keep doing you. (He likes you, remember?) But factor in, alongside your own, *his* needs and wants as well.

3. Respect His Individuality

Respecting the likes and dislikes of the man in your life is just as important as him respecting yours. Consider his preferences. His personality. Take them into account when making shared decisions that affect the two of you, and don't take it personal or get frustrated when they differ from yours. Don't turn your nose up to what gets him excited. Remember that you always have a choice of whether or not to be with someone. If his personality traits or relationship preferences don't jibe with yours, no worries, just move on. The two of you just simply aren't a good fit. But, by no means, try to change him or resent him for being who he is. (Especially if you knew who and how he was from the very beginning.) Requiring his best and then assessing him includes making a determination about how well that works for you.

4. Be a Pal

So, you don't like hockey. Me neither. But he does. Would it kill you to learn the basics of the game via a quick YouTube video? When you understand the game you can enjoy it better, which comes in handy if you live together and only have one TV. Does he have a blooming botany obsession? Don't know your thistle chrysanthemum from your silk plant? Get your 'Google on'. Be a friend to him. Know a little about what he likes. Know enough to talk to him about it if only for a few minutes should he wish to engage you in a little conversation. He might want someone to make mention to about it, and if you are the one who's around then that's you. Resist rolling your eyes up in your *had-it-up-to-here-with-his-dumb-hobby* head. Share a little in his enthusiasm if it doesn't ail you too much. At a minimum, don't make him feel bad for wanting to watch a little *Pruning Wars*.

5. Be Comfortable with Being Inconvenienced

If you're looking for a set-up where you are never inconvenienced or in a situation where you must go out of your way from time to time, then here are some things to consider.

Partnerships and relationships inherently contain some degree of inconvenience at certain times. For example, at some time point in your future or current life, you'll find that taking your child around to all of their practices, appointments, and events can be quite "inconvenient" for you at times. However, the benefits to your child far outweigh any level of discomfort or inconvenience you may otherwise be tempted to complain about.

Well, it's almost the same thing with the man in your life. We can't make a habit of complaining about how we are inconvenienced by having to *(fill in the blank)* for him, or with him. We should, instead, focus on the blessing that is being part of this person's life. We can always choose a personal life where nobody bothers us or asks us to do anything or wants us to come with them anywhere. This life is called *single life*, which isn't a bad thing at all. However, if you are looking for a partnership be prepared to experience the occasional "inconveniences". And if you've chosen your man properly, if you've assessed him accurately, the benefits of being with him should far outweigh the temporary inconveniences of taking one for the team.

There. Those are the basics of how to treat your good man like he's a good man. Keep in mind these basic expressions of love and respect will ensure that you are not only being fair to the man in your life, but that you'll continue receiving all that good loving that he's been giving you.

Part 6
Conclusion

Now We're Making the
Right Choices

Oh, the refreshing feeling of a fresh start.

Take Those Pants Off And Put Your Bra Back On!

Congratulations!

You've done it! You're out of those pants and rocking your bra, ready to make the most of your love life—this time, the *right* way! Should you ever find yourself tempted to unsnap that double-cup wonder and jump back into those tragic trousers, pick up this book again—do some highlighting this go-round—and repeat after me:

"I will take off my pants and keep them off. I will put my bra back on and keep it on. I am a woman, and I deserve and *demand* to be treated like a lady. No exceptions!"

You've arrived. And you look darn good in that dress of yours.

All the best.

-T. L. Brown

A Final Word About Those Pants

Beware of the Seamsters, Tailors, and Personal Shoppers

Did someone else put those pants on you?

Some men, they just don't bring out the best in us. They bring out the *butch* in us.

You could be one of the sexiest, classiest, most beautiful women the world has ever seen, oozing estrogen out of your ears! The most ultra-feminine being walking upright. And yet you almost want to grab your crotch and spit tobacco when you get around this guy. These are some of the most toxic men of all because they are natural repellants to you and your womanhood. Your inner womanly compass is telling you—spinning off the charts, screaming—that something is off about this dude. That your specific brand of chemistry is highly reactive, and dangerously combustible in the worst way. These aren't fireworks you're feeling. They are flares from hell. You won't even *feel* like a woman around him. (Which is downright scary!) Here's the thing:

He put those pants on you.

Some guys are so bitchy they make us butchy.

Now he might be feeling the same way in reverse about you and your energy and how it affects him, but this book isn't about him. He can read someone else's book if he wants to read all about how your energy slides satin thongs up and over his hairy hips. We're talking about what *he* gives off and how it affects *you*. Now, it could be that he's simply a masculinity-challenged male, however your romantic radar and personal preferences define that. Or it could also be that your natal moons don't mix. Who knows?! Better yet, *who cares?!* All you need to know and care about is that he's not the guy you need to be around. That there is something in his energy that is inherently repulsive to you. He'll notice it too, and will even be bitchily-bothered by it, not understanding his culpability in how this woeful role reversal could've occurred. But just remember, he not only put those pants on you, he tailored them, zipped them up, and buckled the belt around them!

Don't macho-walk another millisecond in his defeminizing aura. Take your uterus and ovaries elsewhere.

A Little Something for My Star Savvy Sisters

A Note About Astrological Synastry

For my girls out there unafraid to peek at their horoscopes and peruse their natal charts, I've come to realize that my Sun in the lovely sign of Libra and my marvelous Moon in tantalizing Taurus just doesn't do it for every man. (Those of us who are more "astrology proficient" know it's really more about the natal aspects in our synastry but humor me.) Now that doesn't mean that my Libra/Taurus combo isn't kick-ass. Or that my Libra Rising is falling. It just means it may not be a certain man's match made in heaven. Same with you and your *"It's a No-Go Beau"*. Maybe your moons don't mesh. Be good with that. Let go of a losing combination and move on to a more promising cosmic connection.

Out of the Mouths of Males

Sure. I'd say it's rather customary for men to pay for dates. I mean, no girl wants a cheap guy. Right? -Matthew

If a woman seems too anxious to get my attention, I begin to wonder what's wrong with her. - Elijah

Chicks with rules rule! - Mateo

I honestly don't care what a woman wears when she goes out with me, as long as I get to look at her. - Connor

If she lets me get away with it, why not? - Logan

Bonus

Mini-Book

Take Those Pants Off And Put Your Bra Back On!

How to Find a Quality Love in Two Easy Lessons

Love Lesson #1

Look before you leap.

Love Lesson #2

Look longer!

Thank you so much for reading this book. It is my privilege to share nuggets of wisdom with my fellow woman when it comes to appropriately dealing with men in this modern world of dating. I hope you enjoyed reading. If you did, please kindly leave a review on Amazon.com. By spreading the word you help even more women like us master the art of taking their pants off and putting their bras back on and demanding some good old-fashioned chivalry in their love lives!

All The Best

T. L. Brown